Bob Fosse's Broadway

Bob Fosse's Broadway

Margery Beddow

HEINEMANN
PORTSMOUTH, NH

Heinemann
A division of Reed Elsevier Inc.
361 Hanover Street
Portsmouth, NH 03801-3912
Offices and agents throughout the world

Photo credits may be found on p. 77.

Library of Congress Cataloging-in-Publication Data
Beddow, Margery.
    Bob Fosse's Broadway / Margery Beddow.
      p. cm.
    ISBN 0-435-07002-9
    1. Fosse, Bob, 1927–1987. 2. Choreographers—United States—Biography.
    3. Musicals—United States—History. I. Title.
    GV1785.F67B43 1996
    792.8'2'092—dc20
    [B]   96-10858
                                             CIP

Editor: Lisa A. Barnett
Production: J. B. Tranchemontagne
Manufacturing: Louise Richardson
Cover Design: Barbara Werden

Printed in the United States of America on acid-free paper
04   DA 6 5

Dedicated to the dearest person in my life,
my daughter, Pamela Saunders

Contents

Foreword

With this collection of photos and her lucid text, Margery Beddow has encapsulated the energy and artistry of Bob Fosse. As a member of the cast of *All That Jazz*, a film loosely based on Fosse's life, I observed at firsthand this brilliant and charismatic choreographer at work and play. I was not a trained dancer. It was all new to me. It was the most physically difficult thing I've ever done in my career. I limped through the film and came out with a more than healthy respect for the dancer's craft.

So enthusiastic and electric was Mr. Fosse's choreography that his troupe and I would have danced through a brick wall if he had asked us. I'm certain this only happens when the dancer or the actor is *convinced* that he or she will never look better than when they go through that wall.

Look carefully at these photos. These contorted bodies are alive with erotic beauty. Mr. Fosse's choreography has an infallible sense of line. He offers an audience more pure joy per bar of music than they could ever expect.

Margery Beddow's book is an essential addition to the record of American dance. It places Bob Fosse among its foremost innovators. I thank her for that.

Roy Scheider

Prologue

ob Fosse had a rakish air, and he was definitely dangerous. He'd look out from under his eyebrows, his cigarette a smoke screen between him and the rest of the world, and nobody knew what he was thinking. When I first met Fosse in 1958, he reminded me of a young Frank Sinatra. They both were slightly built and stood with a kind of sunken chest and rather hunched shoulders. Fosse usually wore some sort of hat or cap and always had a cigarette dangling from the corner of his mouth. He was very quiet, but you felt an underlying tension about him all the time. In every rehearsal, it was always very clear how he felt about you or the step or the way you were executing it. He was not afraid to express his anger and everyone knew it. This made you feel a bit on edge or, to say the very least, raised your adrenaline level. Luckily, when he was pleased, his enthusiasm was also immediate and contagious. As time went on he became a bit easier on his performers, but he always remained tough, demanding, and relentless. A compelling presence.

Bob Fosse was one of Broadway's most creative choreographer/directors, and a major force in American musical theater. I was fortunate enough to work with him in the original Broadway productions of *Redhead*, *The Conquering Hero*, and *Little Me*, and later performed leading roles on tour in three more Fosse musicals: *The Pajama Game*, *Damn Yankees*, and *Sweet Charity*. His choreography was so effective and the way in which he worked was so inspiring that people who were in his shows constantly talk about how he made them perform better than they ever thought possible. This book is a firsthand account, based on my own experience and on interviews with many other performers, of what it was like to work with him.

I would like to express my thanks for all the help and encouragement I received from Gwen Verdon. I'd also like to thank the many other people I interviewed for the book, including Roy Scheider, Donna McKechnie, Swen Swenson, Kathryn Doby, Buzz Miller, Graciela Daniele, John Sharp, Ann Reinking, Gene Foote, Elaine Cancilla, John Mineo, Mimi Quillin, Michael Sinclair, Harvey Evans, Kevin Carlisle, Barbara Sharma, David Gold, Alice Evans, Dick Korthaze, Zoya Leporska, Neil Simon, Fred Werner, Stephanie Pope, Lloyd Culbreath, Louise Quick, Eddie Gasper, Chet Walker, and Barry McNabb.

Bob Fosse's Broadway

The Pajama Game

*B*ob Fosse's first big splash as a choreographer on Broadway was in *The Pajama Game,* which was codirected by George Abbott and Jerome Robbins. Richard Adler and Jerry Ross wrote the music and lyrics, and Richard Bissell and George Abbott collaborated on the book. (Bissell had written the best-selling novel *Seven and a Half Cents* from which the plot was taken.) Frederick Brisson was one of the producers. Two young stage managers who were working on the hit *Wonderful Town* ventured into producing (for the first time) along with him. Their names were Robert E. Griffith and Harold S. Prince, and with *The Pajama Game* they sure picked a winner.

The Pajama Game opened on May 13, 1954, and ran until November 24, 1956, a total of 1,063 performances. It was an enormous hit. It could have run even longer if a booking jam-up at the St. James Theater hadn't forced the show to close so that *Li'l Abner* could open. *The Pajama Game* starred John Raitt, Janis Paige, Eddie Foy Jr., and Carol Haney. The show is about the difficulties between labor and management in a pajama factory and about the romantic problems between the superintendent of the factory (Raitt) and the woman who heads the union's griev-ance committee (Paige). The subplot concerns the relationship between the company president's secretary (Haney) and a time-study man (Foy).

Jerome Robbins was originally offered the job of choreogra-pher, but he'd just finished a film in Los Angeles and was exhausted. He told Abbott he'd stage the songs if he got credit as codirector and if he could bring in Bob Fosse to choreograph the dance numbers. Abbott hesitated at first, but Robbins assured him he'd back up Fosse if necessary. (It wasn't, of course.) Fosse, for his part, agreed to do the show only if he got full credit as choreographer and only if he could bring in Carol Haney.

Carol Haney was a fabulous dancer who had been Fosse's partner in the film *Kiss Me Kate*. (Rent it if you get the chance.) The choreographer of the film let Bob choreograph his own duo with Haney, and you can see, even that early in his career, how much sharper and electric his section of the number is than the rest of the choreography.

In *Pajama Game*, Haney did two of the biggest showstoppers: "Hernando's Hideaway," with Raitt and the entire company, and "Steam Heat," with two very well-known and sensational dancers, Buzz Miller and Peter Gennaro.

When Haney sang "Hernando's Hideaway" to Raitt, she used dramatically overdone gestures in the exaggerated style of a vamp from silent films. They arrived at the nightclub in complete darkness; different groups lit matches to direct the audience's attention to each unfolding vignette. Already Fosse was aware of how important lighting was in moving the focus where he wanted it. Throughout his career he continued to make dynamic use of lighting effects. The number also showed his great sense of humor about sexual games. For example, after each dance section, one guy, looking very lost, would wander around in the dark. Holding aloft a lit match, he called out to his girlfriend in a forlorn voice, "Poopsie . . . Poopsie!"

In choreographing "Steam Heat," Fosse really found his own style. This type of trio dance, with its forward thrust of the hips, hunched shoulders, turned-in feet, and sharp, jazzy movements, would become a trademark of his work. Sound effects, derbies, and white gloves were other recurring stylistic elements Fosse first used in this number. One of the tricky aspects to learning the number is incorporating the rhythms and *psss* sounds into the song and dance. To give an example of how detailed his work was, Fosse figured out that by putting an *f* rather than a *p* before the *sss* sound, and saying *fsss*, the sound becomes louder and more percussive.

The tricks with the derby took a million repetitions to master. After one double jazz turn, the hat is held very low in one hand and thrown up in a rolling motion to the other hand, which is held very high. The trick is not to look up when you catch it and to leave your lower hand all the way down at the same time.

Fosse couldn't have picked three better dancers than Haney, Miller, and Gennaro. He always did many months of preparation, and he was bursting with ideas when he got into rehearsal with this fine trio. Dancers always appreciate a creative choreographer who has really done his homework, and Fosse's fervor and intensity made his performers eager to get started. And so they went to work. Fosse made you feel as if you were really helping him out, and he was very generous about allowing performers to interject their own ideas. He wanted you to know he respected your opinion, even though he always made the final decision.

Unbelievably, in the beginning George Abbott wanted to cut this number. One reason Abbott was a great director was that he never wanted anything to slow down the action. He didn't want to give the audience a moment to analyze what was or wasn't happening on stage. Fortunately, Robbins convinced Abbott to leave Fosse's "Steam Heat" alone. It stopped the show every night and became one of his most famous numbers.

Haney had worked with Fosse in Hollywood, where she had also been Gene Kelly's assistant. She won many awards for her portrayal of Gladys, but she somehow never felt she deserved all the acclaim. Accident-prone, she broke her ankle doing a jump on an uneven bed in the "Jealousy Ballet" shortly after the opening. Her understudy, Shirley MacLaine, had to go on, and as luck would have it, the movie producer Hal B. Wallis was out front. He brought MacLaine to Paramount, where she made her first film, Alfred Hitchcock's *The Trouble with Harry*. And that, my dears, (as if you didn't know) is how that particular star was born. Zoya Leporska, Fosse's assistant on *Pajama Game*, told me that when she said to MacLaine in understudy rehearsal, "Let's learn it, Shirley" (meaning the "Steam Heat" number), MacLaine replied, "Aw, when am I ever going to do it?"

Many years after the Broadway run of *The Pajama Game*, in the last summer tour that starred John Raitt in his original role, I got to play Gladys. I also choreographed the show, except for "Steam Heat." Fosse gave me permission to use the original choreography for that number. Frank Derbas, who understudied Miller and Gennaro on Broadway, was nice enough to teach it to me. There is so much intensity and exactness in the movement that it is an exhausting number. But it works so well and is so funny that it was wonderful to get the chance to do it. In dancing the number, I found the danger is in getting faster and not keeping the beat together. The trio has to feel like one person. Fosse loved using different percussive rhythms, and between clapping our hands, stamping our feet, and making our clucking and *fsss* sounds, we kept ourselves very busy.

One of the humorous aspects of Fosse's choreography was his element of surprise. For instance, if the music states a theme three times, most choreographers repeat the step three times. But Fosse would do the same step only twice. The third time he would do something totally unexpected. I once had a small disaster during a sequence of that type in "Steam Heat." When we came to the third repeat in the music, I almost forgot to change to the new step. Remembering at the last moment, I threw myself into the move, which happened to be a fall to both knees. Ouch! I pulled a few muscles and ligaments that night, but I never again forgot that Fosse's work was always unconventional.

The Pajama Game not only won the Tony Award for Best Musical, Best Composer, and Best Libretto, it also earned Fosse the first of many Tony Awards he would receive for his choreography. In 1957 he also choreographed Stanley Donen's movie version, starring Doris Day, with John Raitt, Carol Haney, and Eddie Foy Jr. in their original roles. Revivals of this show have been mounted many times, and it is still very popular. Its most important contribution, though, was to bring to the world's attention a terrific new choreographer named Bob Fosse.

Damn Yankees

A few years ago, the well-known choreographer Michael Kidd presented Gwen Verdon with an award from the Directors Guild for her restaging of the show *Dancin'*. At the ceremony he told this story: "After Gwen had auditioned for Bob Fosse and George Abbott for *Damn Yankees*, Bob called me up to ask if the rumors that Gwen was difficult were true. I said, 'Gwen is not only very talented and will make your choreography look good, but she will also fight for your material.' Then I added, 'If you want someone who's not difficult, hire my sister.' Fosse decided to hire Gwen Verdon."

Damn Yankees was the first time Bob Fosse worked with Gwen Verdon. They had seen each other before, when they were both in Hollywood working on different pictures for MGM, and they met once at a party given by Michael Kidd. Fosse was at the party with his wife, Joan McCracken. Gwen had seen Joan in Brecht's *Galileo* (with Charles Laughton), and she told me later that she had idolized Joan—not only because she was a very good dancer, but also because she was such a wonderful actress. Fosse learned a great deal from and was very influenced by both McCracken and Verdon. Joan McCracken died very young, and it was something Fosse never got over.

Damn Yankees opened at the Forty-sixth Street Theater (now called the Richard Rodgers Theater) on May 5, 1955. It was directed by George Abbott, and the book was written by Abbott and Douglas Wallop. The music and lyrics were by Richard Adler and Jerry Ross, and the show was choreographed by Bob Fosse. It was produced by the same people who gave us *The Pajama Game*:

Frederick Brisson, Robert E. Griffith, and Harold S. Prince. The show won six Tony Awards: Best Musical, Best Actress, Best Actor, Best Composer, Best Librettist, and, of course, Best Choreography. It would have won seven Tonys but there was no separate award for director of a musical until 1960.

Damn Yankees is the story of a middle-aged fan of the Washington Senators who sells his soul to the devil so he can be transformed into a young, wonderful baseball player named Joe Hardy and help beat those "damn Yankees." Because he's in real estate, he knows enough to include an escape clause in his contract. The devil, however, has a very tempestuous assistant named Lola whose job is to make sure he doesn't use it.

Fosse asked Verdon to work with him before the entire company started rehearsals, and she agreed. They met at a place called Walton's Warehouse for their first rehearsal together on "Whatever Lola Wants." Fosse had a habit of exhaling through his nose a lot when he was feeling edgy. So with flared and whitened nostrils pouring smoke, he stood in front of Verdon and said, "I'm very nervous." Gwen told me she replied, "S-S-S-So am I." Little did they realize what musical comedy history they were going to make together.

In "Whatever Lola Wants," Lola does a very intense stalking step toward Joe. After three incisive steps, she notices an itch on the back of one calf. She suddenly switches her attention from going after Joe to scratching the back of one leg with her toe, then just as quickly returns to her stalking step. Fosse did it perfectly, but Verdon was having some difficulty keeping her balance. She explained to him that it was perfectly understandable because she was wearing very high heels. The next day Fosse arrived at rehearsal with a box under his arm. He said to Verdon, "I never ask people to do what I'm not willing to do myself." He then sat down, put on a pair of oversize high heels, and showed her how the step should be done.

"Whatever Lola Wants" worked so well because of Fosse's ever-humorous attitude toward sex in the number. Lola had been the ugliest woman in Providence, Rhode Island, before she sold her soul to the devil, so this was her convoluted idea of how to vamp the young baseball hero. Lola thought it would be hot to pretend to be Spanish, and Fosse incorporated every trick he remembered from his early days as a performer working with strippers in clubs. Throwing off her gloves and hat, Lola slithered out of her skirt and nonchalantly dropped it over Joe's head. Sitting on the floor, she walked backwards on her hips, sliding out of her pantslip (this was a half slip with legs). After beating the floor and swinging the pantslip in a circle over her head, she threw them backward at Joe from between her legs. She shook her boobs, threw her arms around him, crawled under his knees, played peeka-boo, pretended to phone him, pretended to shoot him, tantalizing him in every way possible. It was hysterical, and for my money one of the funniest vamp numbers ever created.

Fosse had completed all of Lola's choreography before company rehearsals began, but two more numbers ("A Little Brains, A Little Talent" and "Who's Got the Pain When They Do the Mambo?") were added for her during the pre-Broadway tour. When Abbott and the rest of the creative staff saw how incredible Verdon was in the role, they began to give her more and more to do. The producers also changed the big poster in the advertising from one with a generic baseball motif to the famous standing-astride picture of Verdon.

One afternoon at a rehearsal in New Haven, Verdon was handed the music to "A Little Brains, A Little Talent." Abbott, Adler, and Ross asked her how long it would take her to memorize it. Noting the many verses and choruses, all of them full of inside rhymes, she said it looked quite difficult. Then she asked how long it would take them to complete the orchestrations. They said they could get it on that very night. Verdon had only a few hours to learn the number, and there was no time left over to stage it. George Abbott said, "Oh, just take the stage, kid. Just take the stage like Ethel Merman." Verdon went to Fosse in tears: "I don't know what he's talking about!" Fosse said, "Don't worry, I'll fix it, I'll fix it." And he did, with some of the wittiest and most subtle movement ever. When he had finished, Verdon showed the number to Adler and Ross. Ross loved it, but Adler stammered, "Can't you make the bumps . . . bigger . . . badder . . . better?" Verdon said, "Which one?" And he said, "Bigger!" Verdon replied, "Actually, I don't do any bumps in this number." (Fosse had told her to be very tiny in her movement, like she was adjusting herself inside her panties, moving nothing but her hips.) So Adler said, "Well, you know, when you sling your rear end over to the right, my friends don't know what you're doing." Verdon began to boil at being talked to in such a derogatory manner. You could have cut the air with a knife. Gwen finally replied with a few well-chosen expletives ending with, "And, *my friends* think it's terrific!" To break the tension, Fosse walked nonchalantly between them and murmured over his shoulder, "You heard the lady!"

Fosse's style was much more difficult to pick up than one might suppose. When he started out as a tap dancer in clubs, some of the great old-timers from burlesque were still performing. He picked up many wonderful vaudeville bits from them, which he passed along to his dancers: head and foot sculls (to show astonishment at something someone has said or done, make your whole body go stiff, which makes your head or foot quiver); double and triple takes (look slowly at something, then look away, then look back very quickly once or twice); the unhinged lower arm (bring the right elbow up even with the shoulder, let the lower part of the arm hang down and swing a bit like a pendulum, now bat the right hand with the left hand, causing it to swing in a circle going from down to up and around); and many old hat-and-cane routines. Fosse was also influenced by Jack Cole. Cole was a renowned choreographer from Broadway and film, who has been called the father of American jazz dance. But unlike Cole, who worked more in plié and into the floor, Fosse preferred to stretch a movement up to its maximum, and he loved to jump. Although his natural stance was rather round-shouldered, Fosse loved to lift the chest up high when doing steps with an optimistic feel. He was influenced by Jerome Robbins, too. Of course, Fosse had his own sexy, funny, eccentric style. We used to say it took a dancer an entire season in one of his shows to feel at ease with his way of dancing.

Some of the steps in "Who's Got the Pain?" were not only difficult, they were truly original. When Lola sings out, "Is there a doctor in the house?" Verdon had only four beats in which to put one foot on her partner's thigh, throw the other leg over his shoulder, and end up sitting on one side of his neck. Then after repeating the line, she again had only four beats to throw the leg (now down her partner's back) over his other shoulder and, as he bent forward, lean back until she was hanging upside down by her knees. In this position she delivered the line, "If there's a doctor in the house . . ." a third time and then, in one beat, as her partner straightened up, she sat back up on his shoulders and sang, "point him out."

In another famous step from that number, Lola and her mambo partner stood back to back and, holding their backs together, both bent their knees until they were sitting on the floor. Then, while pressing the backs of their necks together, they raised their hips off the floor and walked their feet out until they made a straight line from their knees to their shoulders. Holding this position by pressing their necks and shoulders together, they then both walked stage right (with their hats down over their eyes). At the proper moment, they lifted their hats to say, "Errrp!" The step isn't easy to do, and you have to make little razor slices in the soles of your sneakers in order not to slip, but the look is very funny, and audiences love it.

I got to play Lola when a producer of a stock company asked Verdon to suggest someone for the role. I was understudying Verdon in *Redhead* at the time, and I was so surprised and pleased when she recommended me. Not only that, but she came over to my apartment and told me all kinds of secrets about how to do the part. I auditioned the next day and, thanks to Gwen's coaching, I got the job. One of the boys in our show (Erik Kristen) had been in *Damn Yankees*, and he began to show me the original choreography. When Gwen discovered me working by myself on stage before our show, she proceeded to refine and polish whatever number I was rehearsing. Not only that, but Richard Kiley came to my dressing room one night and said, "You know, Margie, I always wanted to do Joe Hardy. Could I rehearse some of those scenes with you?" I said, "Are you kidding? You're Richard Kiley!" (For you youngsters, he played opposite Gwen in *Redhead* and is quite a famous actor.) Talk about being lucky. Here I had Kiley to rehearse with me, and Verdon to work with me on the part.

Fosse had been away from our tour for a while, but one night before our performance, when I was going over "Whatever Lola Wants" on stage, I saw a little movement in the darkened wings. I peered a bit closer, and my heart dropped when I realized it was Fosse. God, I realized I hadn't even asked him for permission to do his choreography yet. I started trying to apologize and explain all at the same time, and the words came out a garbled mess. When I finally stopped talking, Bob just gave me that little half-smile of his next to his cigarette, and said, "No, that's O.K., keep going. I like to watch it again."

So, feeling my pulse throbbing away in my neck, I began again. I was all dirty and sweaty, and there was no music. Fosse had just married the real Lola about two months ago. I was sure he was thinking, "This is hopeless," but he just started working with me, giving me images and subtext for each step.

He'd say things like, "Now feel like a fat girl doing that step," or "This pose has the same feeling as the Petty-girl poses in the famous calendar." Every step had a thought behind it. I feel this is one of the reasons why Fosse's dances were always so mesmerizing to watch: dancers weren't just doing movements, they had a whole life going on underneath the choreography. They were always thinking something, not just moving around like robots (like so many hip-hop and calisthenic dancers look like today). One of my favorite Fosse quotes is, "You can't be a good dancer unless you're a good actor. Otherwise it's all just so much animated wallpaper!"

Fosse's attention to detail was well known by every dancer who ever worked for him. When he used that pose with elbows held tightly in to the body, hands open out to the sides, he'd always say the energy didn't end at the hands: he wanted such intensity that it would feel like light was streaming from every finger. When he gave Liza Minnelli that pose as part of the title song in the movie *Cabaret*, he used a lighting effect that made it look like light really *was* streaming from each finger.

I feel extremely lucky not only to have done the role of Lola, but also to have had all that help from both Fosse and Verdon. They were both so generous in sharing their knowledge with me, and Fosse's choreography was truly extraordinary.

New Girl in Town

*L*ike *The Pajama Game* and *Damn Yankees, New Girl in Town* was directed by George Abbott and choreographed by Bob Fosse. Also for the third time, the producers were Frederick Brisson, Robert E. Griffith, and Harold S. Prince. The show opened at the Forty-sixth Street Theater on May 14, 1957. Quite astoundingly, it was based on the Pulitzer Prize–winning play *Anna Christie*, written by Eugene O'Neill in 1922. At this time both Verdon and Fosse were heavily into Sandy Meisner's acting technique, and I'm sure they were very interested in doing some serious dramatic work. Meisner was a very famous and excellent acting teacher. However, O'Neill could be considered a rather gloomy choice for a musical, especially one to be directed by George Abbott, someone who has always been known for his razzmatazz and his snappy shows. Abbott tried to liven things up by changing the time of the play from 1922 to 1900, a period in which clothes and decor were prettier. It was undoubtedly a good idea to make the show more colorful, but it was still far from comedy.

The show turned out to be quite successful on Broadway, and ran for over a year before it went on a national tour. There were problems in the beginning, though, because not only was the source material so "nonmusical," but the collaborators each had such a different vision on how to present the piece. (I believe this helped Fosse decide that the next time out, he was going to direct as well as choreograph.)

Everyone says that Gwen Verdon's portrayal of the title role was unforgettable. The part was so difficult, they had to split her understudy between two people, one to do the acting and singing and another to do the dancing. Brooks Atkinson wrote in his review, "Verdon gives a complete characterization from the slut to the woman—common in manner, but full of pride, disillusioned, but willing to believe, a woman of silence and mysteries. It would be an affecting job on any stage. Amid the familiar diversions of a Broadway musical jamboree, it is sobering and admirable." Verdon won the Tony Award for Best Actress in a Musical.

The musical's story line is a harsh waterfront tale of a prostitute named Anna who is trying to live down her past. She has quit working in a Midwest brothel (after a bout with tuberculosis) and returned to her home in New York. Here she has a tender reunion with her father (Cameron Prud'homme), who is the captain of a barge. Neither her father nor Matt, the young Irishman (George Wallace) who falls in love with her has any idea of her unsavory past. That is, until the beer-guzzling, blowzy mistress (costar Thelma Ritter) of Anna's father lets the cat out of the bag. From all accounts, Ritter might have stolen the show if it hadn't been for Verdon's incredible performance. In the musical adaptation, Anna's young man leaves for a whole year at sea before he at last decides to return and forgive her. In O'Neill's play, it only took the man two days. Perhaps they needed more time to show off all that wonderful dancing.

The words and music were by the Tin Pan Alley composer Bob Merrill. At one time Merrill had a contract to write the music for a song-and-dance film, also based on O'Neill's *Anna Christie,* called (are you ready?) *A Saint She Ain't.* Even though the film was never made, Merrill was able to get Abbott interested in doing the project as a Broadway musical.

The opening number, "Roll Yer Socks Up," showcased the men in the chorus as longshoremen and sailors. They did very strong movement with great gusto and masculinity, getting the show off to an exciting and vigorous start.

Later on, in the dance section of "Ain't No Flies On Me," Harvey Evans (one of the dancers) told me that Fosse, as usual, taught the steps to everyone before deciding who would be featured in the number. Eddie Phillips (a wildly funny and awesome dancer) was ultimately one of the men featured, and did a section that had these slipping, sliding, camel-walk steps that Eddie did so well. As his solo expanded, it turned comedic and became an ode to a mug of beer.

Another memorable number was "The Check Apron Ball," involving all the dancers, but one section featured a highly stylized and successful soft-shoe performed by Gwen Verdon, Harvey Evans, and Harvey Jung. In the middle of the number Verdon had a solo unlike anything ever seen before on Broadway. It was called the pony dance and started very simply and slowly with finger snaps and small touch steps. At one point she released her hair, which had been held up with one hairpin. As it cascaded down, she began to flip her hair front and back and around in circles. In this dance, Fosse began using a device that would become another trademark. Dancers did a step across the front of the stage, and after they exited, they would tear around backstage, behind the backdrop, and reappear on the other side at the end of the line. The effect was a never-ending line of people. (Every time one very heavyset fellow went across, the audience recognized him and laughed and applauded like crazy.) This dance built slowly into a cakewalk using all the dancers. At the height of the number, the curtain slowly descended for intermission. Fifteen minutes later as the curtain rose for the second act, the dancers were still cakewalking madly away as if they had never stopped.

One of the most important moments in the show was the "Whorehouse Ballet." Matt (George Wallace) stood stage left against the proscenium and imagined what Anna's life must have been like as a prostitute. Of course he had it terribly wrong, but the ballet was about the lascivious thoughts going on in his head. John Aristede, a very masculine and sensual-looking guy, was Verdon's partner, and their interaction was dramatic and extremely sexual. The set consisted of only a few chairs and a staircase. Verdon, at one point, dove off the top of the stairs backwards into Aristede's arms. There was no music, only the throb of a double bass, which made everything very intense. At the very end of the dance, Aristede had Verdon in a backbend over his shoulder, only holding on to her foot in the front as he carried her lifeless form off the stage. The producers and George Abbott thought it was all too strong and wanted the number redone or at least toned down. Fighting with producers over what he believed should be in the show was a recurring element in Fosse's career. Verdon was sensational in the ballet, and Fosse refused to cut it.

One day during the New Haven run a mother and her teenage daughter saw the show. The mother was so shocked that she brought a policeman (who was really only a crossing guard) backstage to complain that the "Whorehouse Ballet" was indecent and pornographic. This gave Abbott a reason during the move from New Haven to Boston to cut the ballet and have the staircase removed and burned. The cast didn't realize the number was cut and the set was gone until they arrived in Boston for the opening. The number was not put back in the show until about a month after the Broadway opening. Gwen fought and fought to have it restored. Fosse finally had a whole orchestration made (which made it less sensual) and rechoreographed it without the staircase. It was finally put back in the show on June 23, which was Fosse's birthday. For the upcoming retrospective of Fosse's work, Verdon told me she is reconstructing the ballet back to its original form.

I think one of the reasons Fosse wanted to do this show was because he was definitely fascinated by the darker side of life. There was always a feeling of danger when you were around him. Some of his most interesting productions involved very frightening characters. Think of the title character of the movie *Lenny*, and the murderer in *Star 80*. And many of his shows and films were about someone who was able to survive in spite of being in dire situations. Look at the leads not only in *New Girl in Town*, but also in *Damn Yankees, Sweet Charity, Cabaret, Chicago,* and *Big Deal*. This dangerous side to Fosse gave a menacing and exciting edge to his shows.

Fosse loved to use very decided types in his shows. In addition to the sexy, darker types and offbeat character dancers, he favored dancers who looked very young and innocent, such as Harvey Evans, Barbara Sharma, Louise Quick, and Kevin Carlisle. Both Evans and Sharma told me that when they auditioned for Fosse, he asked them if they were old enough to be working. (Though they were both about seventeen, they looked twelve.) He always got a kick out of watching young dancers like this doing his funny, sophisticated, and sexy moves.

Fosse's steps may sometimes have seemed simple, but they were much harder than they looked. And his insistence on strength in the movement and intensity in the hands always made the dance so much more dynamically expressive. He wanted his dancers not only to get all the many rhythms and moves exactly as he did them, but also to fill out the movement with their own personality. He'd watch what each dancer brought to the movement and then, after removing all the excess baggage, he'd use what was intrinsically right. Many of his dancers have told me they felt Fosse was letting them help him create, and this certainly gave an excitement and spontaneity to the work. He would always explain the circumstances of the scene, so that the dancers would understand what was needed in the moment. Even though Fosse had a definite vocabulary of steps, the style of every show he did was unique. He pushed harder and asked for more than anyone ever thought possible to give, but somehow each performer dug a little deeper and gave Fosse what he wanted.

One night Jack Cole came to see the show. Verdon had been Cole's assistant for many years, and I'm sure she was quite happy to know he was out front. Fosse was also pleased, as he was quite an admirer of Cole's work. The dancers too were all excited that Cole would be watching their performance. It was definitely an electric evening. After the show, as the dancers watched from one of the dressing room windows upstairs, Fosse, Verdon, and Cole left the theater and walked together down Forty-sixth Street. Harvey Evans said everyone felt not only extremely lucky to be working with these people, but also as though these three were the cream of Broadway passing before their very eyes.

Redhead

*R*edhead was the third show Gwen Verdon did with Bob Fosse, and she told me it was her favorite. It was my first audition for a Fosse show. He was becoming quite renowned for his showstopping choreography, and four hundred or more female dancers showed up for the audition. When I saw all the people, I anticipated chaos, but Fosse always gave the fairest and most organized auditions I ever attended. He taught everyone three different combinations and would grade each dancer A to E on each one—and the best part was that he actually based his decisions on the grades. He had a great eye for seeing who was right for a show. It didn't matter how well you knew him or how many shows you had already done with him. If your card wasn't in the group of cards that carried the best marks at the end of the audition, you just weren't called back.

After waiting on pins and needles for a seemingly endless number of days, I finally got the call to come to the final audition. At the end of that exhausting day, there were ten girls left, and he needed nine (eight dancers and a "swing"). The swing girl understudied all the girls in the chorus. This is the combination he gave us to help him decide who to keep: changement into a grand plié and, from the deepest part of the plié, jump up into an air split, landing in fifth position. Twice. (If you're not a dancer, ask a dancer to show you how this combination would look.) It's a true test of strength. Since I was just emerging from six years with ballet companies and had never been stronger in my life, I managed to get the show.

At the end of the audition, Gwen Verdon walked in to meet everyone. Her hair was flame red, and her skin was so white and luminous it looked like a light was glowing inside her. The effect was breathtaking. She was very charming and gracious to all of us. (She had more discipline than just about anybody, and talk about being in good shape, one day in rehearsal, I put my hand on her shoulder—it was like putting my hand on a marble statue.)

Redhead, starring Gwen Verdon and Richard Kiley, opened at the Forty-sixth Street Theater on February 5, 1959. It was written by Herbert and Dorothy Fields, Sidney Sheldon, and David Shaw. The music was by Albert Hague and the lyrics were by Dorothy Fields. Fosse was for the first time the director as well as the choreographer. The show ran for more than a year and won seven Tony Awards. As Dorothy Fields wrote, "*Redhead* is part Agatha Christie and part Keystone comedy, and a very romantic murder-mystery musical." The show takes place in Edwardian London. Essie Whimple (Verdon) makes wax figures for a museum. She also has visions— she sees the face of the strangler who has been terrorizing the city. The show is all about mistaken identity, trapping the killer, and the romance between Essie and the handsome Strong Man from the local Odeon Theater (Kiley), who helps save her.

What a revelation it was to work with Fosse and Verdon! I had been under the mistaken impression that people in shows didn't work as hard as people in ballet companies. It certainly wasn't true where these two were concerned. Fosse would work at the Variety Arts Studios for at least six months before rehearsals started for any of his shows. Verdon worked so intensely that Fosse was always telling her to take it easy and not dance so hard.

One of the things that amazed me about Fosse was his willingness to edit his own work. He had no ego about it. If we didn't get the step right away or it didn't look exactly right to him, he immediately wanted to change it or just cut the whole thing. Verdon was always asking him to give us just a few more tries to make it work. He was also willing to cut big sections or even a whole dance if it didn't match his vision of it. I've watched him redo a whole number in a few hours when the first version didn't work. That's when all the homework he had done on each number paid off. Somewhere in his mind he always had Plan B to go to.

In those days you could be fired at the end of the first three days of rehearsal with no notice. (Maybe you still can.) At the beginning of the third day, Bob asked three of the dancers to step out into the hall with him. The rest of us held our breath thinking he was going to fire them on the spot. But all he did was give them a warning. They had that last day to prove themselves, and they all made sure they did it. Most of Fosse's dancers were fiercely loyal and proud to be picked for one of his shows. He demanded everything from us, and we did impossible things we had no idea we could do. (I remember singing and dancing one number where we held a long note even after flying through the air and being caught in a lift.) We were able to do these things because his expectations were so high. Rehearsals were very hard (to say the least), but we believed in him so much, we'd try anything to produce *whatever* he wanted on the stage.

Because *Redhead* was Fosse's debut as a director, he decided to rehearse the dancers by themselves for the first three weeks. That way he had the choreography pretty much finished before the rest of the company came in. Although Fosse knew exactly what he wanted from the actors, I think he was a bit nervous about verbalizing it. The last day of our dance rehearsals Fosse said to us, "Now tomorrow all those actors are going to come in here, and they're going to want to know what their motivation is. The first actor who asks that, I want you to all stand up together and say, 'Because Bobby says so!'" Of course the very first day some hapless actor asked, "Why?" The dancers all stood up, and after our unison response and everyone's hysterical laughter, nobody else asked too many questions.

During the out-of-town tryout in Philadelphia, we had a near disaster. In the beginning of the great "Pickpocket Tango," which Verdon danced with Buzz Miller, a jail set was flown in to enclose Verdon and the girls in the chorus. The bars of the jail extended across the entire stage and had to be locked into place on each side of the proscenium. The set was metal and extremely heavy. A stagehand on either side would watch it come in and then secure it. One night one of the stagehands missed his cue. We had all been warned not to pull on the set before the stagehands got a hold of it, so we were slightly upstage as Verdon put her hands up on the bars. Suddenly the entire set fell with a great crash right on top of both of her feet. Verdon fell to the ground holding her toes, and we all made a circle around her to hide her from the audience. I hissed to the stage manager to pull the curtain, but he just looked at me blankly. It was one of those awful moments when you could have driven a truck through the silence on stage and nobody knows what to do. Suddenly, out of the corner of my eye, I saw Fosse come running down the center aisle of the theater. He jumped clear across the orchestra pit, unlocked the jail door, entered the jail, picked Verdon up in his arms, and roared to the stage manager, "Pull the goddamn curtain!" Slowly the curtain came down. Soon we heard the ominous announcement over the public address system, "If there's a doctor in the house, please come to the backstage area."

The entire company was in shock. Everywhere people were crying or swearing or just generally looking scared out of their wits. Three doctors came backstage and examined Verdon's feet. About an hour later (while the audience waited), they decided nothing was broken, and Verdon was able to continue the show wearing a pair of soft slippers under her long costume.

In the very next scene, Kiley said to Verdon, "Now Essie, if you see the killer, stamp your foot three times, like this," and he stamped his foot very hard three times. The audience let out a groan. Verdon tilted her head up to Kiley and said, "Like this?" and daintily lifting her gown to show her ankle, she softly and gingerly tapped her foot three times. The audience stood up and cheered.

The next day the show closed down since Gwen's feet were horribly bruised, she had no understudy, and her standby (Catherine Damon) had recently left the show because of a burst appendix. There was an immediate understudy audition out of the girls in the chorus. Patti Karr, the swing girl, got it. She had somehow not only learned all eight girls' places in numerous numbers, she had also learned Verdon's role. This was all the more amazing because not only was Verdon's role very demanding in every way, but the character was almost never off the stage.

It made me realize how important it is to learn a role whenever you have the opportunity. A year and a half later, when I finally got to understudy the part myself and was feeling pretty nervous about it, Patti said to me rather succinctly, "My only words of advice are, don't fuck around. Learn it." And excellent advice it is too. Fosse told us that whenever you are the under-study, you're responsible for knowing that part completely by the first public performance. Much later, when we'd been on the road with the show for about two weeks, one of the new understudies had to go on, and he kept going blank. With Verdon feeding him his lines under her breath, they some-how got through it, but Fosse was furious. After the show Fosse told the guy he had to know the role by the next understudy rehearsal, which was the next day. We worked with him all night, but there just wasn't enough time for him to be sure of all the lines. At the end of the rehearsal, Fosse fired him. It's a lesson I'll never forget.

Gwen Verdon did a number called "Herbie Fitch's Twitch," which remains in my memory one of the classic funny moments in the show. At this point in the plot she was trying to get into the show-within-the-show by auditioning with a number her father used to do in vaudeville. She had on a tweed suit and a derby hat and carried a cane. The lyric was a real tongue twister, accompanied by very comic moves reminiscent of Charlie Chaplin. Verdon was charming and so very, very funny. The chorus was on stage as the performers at the Odeon Theater, and the hardest part was acting like we thought it was a terrible number.

Verdon had a lovely ballad to sing, "Merely Marvelous," when Essie falls in love with the Strong Man from the Odeon Theater (Kiley). Fosse gave

Verdon a wonderful bit of direction with Kiley, who was smoking a cigar. Just before he left her alone on the stage he exhaled a huge puff of smoke. After his exit she walked into it as if she was being ecstatically embraced by the smoke he left behind.

At the end of the first act, we did a ballet called "Essie's Dream," which lasted about thirty minutes. There have been many long ballets in shows, but this one was unique: we did five different styles of dance. The first section was Fosse's own unique style of jazz. We wore black tights and leotards with white bow ties and white gloves. Our derbies were flown in on a pipe, hanging from wires of various lengths. Each couple went into a different lift and plucked the hats out of what looked to the audience like thin air. One night when I was up in the lift to pluck my derby off the wire, my hair got tangled in the hook that held the derby. As the pipe started to fly back up into the wings, it began to lift me along with it. My partner (David Gold) looked up at me in amazement as he felt me getting lighter and lighter. (Luckily I had on a false bun of hair, which eventually pulled away from my head and disappeared into the flies.)

The second section was a funny, exuberant cancan for Verdon and the girls. One of the girls had to throw herself down in a split and then lean her head flat down over her leg so Gwen could to do a cartwheel over her. One day there was a new dancer in this part. She was so nervous during her first performance that when she put her head down, she did it so violently she broke her nose. Now that's nervous!

The third section was a wild gypsy dance for Verdon and the guys. She made her entrance by jumping, in the wings, off a table onto a trampoline. From the trampoline she dove onto the stage, where three boys caught her in a very high horizontal lift. It was a sensational entrance. From there they all went into a furiously complicated tambourine dance.

The fourth section was a snappy march performed by all the dancers. We did military movements, with lots of intricate formations. This turned into a long serpentine of many big jumps. At the end, all seventeen of us did a double inside turn into a swastika jump, turning in the air into a fall and tight body roll, and ending in a salute on one knee. If anyone miscalculated where he or she was supposed to land (and sometimes we did), there could easily be a terrible collision. We all made a pact not to drink before the show and to promise to tell if we did, because you could kill someone if you didn't have all your senses intact and landed in someone else's spot. (When someone did confess, that person was thrown in a cold shower and made to drink gallons of coffee.)

The fifth and last section was an old-fashioned English music hall number, with all the girls in ruffled dresses and lace pantaloons. The dream is over now for Essie and she's back in the real world of the Odeon Theater. In that section Essie kept going the wrong way and messing up all the choreography. It was planned out so well that the audience kept being surprised and roaring with laughter.

We kept our black leotards and tights on underneath during all the incredibly fast costume changes, which were done in the wings. The music never stopped and neither did the movement—Fosse knew how to slip a few dancers off early in order to be ready to start the next section, so it looked like there were sixty dancers in the chorus instead of sixteen. It was great!

Fosse and Verdon were so much on the same wavelength that they were always talking to each other in shorthand. Fosse would say, "I don't know about this step. What if we—" and Verdon would answer, "That's a good idea, but do you think—" and Fosse would say, "Sure, if everyone will just—" and Verdon would interject, "You don't have to worry about that, I'll be sure to—" and Fosse would answer, "I know you will." They knew what they were talking about, but I'll be damned if anyone else did.

When we went on the road after running for about a year on Broadway, we played the Edwin Lester circuit. (Lester had theaters in Los Angeles and San Francisco, and each year he would pick one of the most successful musicals that was about to close on Broadway to go for a tour of his theaters.) For this tour they added four weeks in Chicago (Fosse's hometown), then six weeks each in Los Angeles and San Francisco. Soon after we arrived in Los Angeles, we did a television show, which Fosse choreographed. All of the girls were in the television studio dressing room with Verdon when she suddenly smiled at me and, putting out her left hand to show me her ring, said, "Look, Margie. Bob and I got married in Chicago." She probably told me first because she knew I'd scream and everyone else would come running, which is exactly what happened. We were all so delighted with the news. It was a wonderful company, and many of us are still very close, even after all these years.

The Conquering Hero

*T*he show Bob Fosse did immediately after *Redhead*'s successful run was *The Conquering Hero* (based on Preston Sturges's movie *Hail the Conquering Hero*, which starred Eddie Bracken). It opened at Broadway's ANTA Theater (now called the Virginia Theater) on January 16, 1961. Moose Charlap and Norman Gimbel wrote the music and lyrics, and Larry Gelbart wrote the book. Gelbart's book was very amusing, but its antiwar message led some reviewers to label it "un-American." (Gelbart later wrote the hit television show *M*A*S*H*, which also had an antiwar theme, and it ran for eleven years. The popularity of war seems to go in cycles, and *The Conquering Hero* was, unfortunately, out of sync with the times.)

The show's protagonist is a young man named Woodrow Truesmith, the son of a World War I hero. During World War II the boy enlists, but at boot camp his hay fever is so bad he has to be discharged. Ashamed to return home, he goes to another town to work in a shipyard and arranges for a buddy to mail home his letters from the South Pacific.

When the war ends, Truesmith, returning home on the train, runs into his Marine buddies from boot camp. They feel sorry for his plight, and, stuffing him into one of their medal-laden uniforms, they call ahead to tell his family of his imminent arrival. The whole town turns out to welcome the conquering hero, and the citizens decide he must run for mayor. During the campaign, the truth finally comes out, and Truesmith confesses to the ruse with great chagrin. Happily, the townspeople are so proud of his honesty that they make him mayor anyway—and naturally, he gets the girl, too.

Robert Tucker and I assisted Fosse on the auditions, and again it was amazing how many people showed up. Everyone wanted to work with Bob Fosse. At the female dance audition the women kept pushing forward so much to see the step (and to be seen), they almost pushed me off the stage. Finally Fosse explained I was there to help them learn the steps.

Fosse had owned the rights to this show for quite some time and had originally planned to produce it himself. He handpicked the entire creative team and, as usual, did months of preproduction work. As rehearsals drew near, however, he began to realize that producing took too much time from choreographing and directing, so he signed over the rights to Robert L. Whitehead and Roger Stevens.

Many of Broadway's most popular and successful musicals were choreographed and directed by one person instead of two. Besides Bob Fosse, there were many other director/choreographers: Jerry Robbins, Michael Bennett, Michael Kidd, and Gower Champion. To me it always seems to work better when one person is in charge. I feel because Fosse had studied with Sandy Meisner and had the most understanding of what acting was all about, he was the best of them all. One of the most difficult things about putting on a musical is getting everyone to collaborate on the same vision of the show. But it is not a democracy—someone has to be responsible for combining all the many facets and making the final decisions. Fosse always tried to be everywhere, supervising every detail. It was the beginning of the era of the director/choreographer, and some people resented the power this gave to one person. It was a strange circumstance since each member of the creative team, except the director or the choreographer, had a union to protect him or her. The writer, the composer, the lyricist, the costume designer, the lighting designer, and the arranger (among others) all had the power to withdraw their work if they weren't happy with the way things were going.

During the pre-Broadway tour, Tucker and I sometimes worked with Fosse in the theater after the show on a new number until the wee small hours, but it was worth it to see how his mind worked. His concentration, energy, and determination were amazing. Much later I learned that some of this amazing energy came from the Dexedrine Fosse was taking. In those days, it was not unusual for dancers to take uppers. It was easy to get a doctor to prescribe amphetamines for weight loss, because nobody knew they were dangerous drugs. Unfortunately, some people got hooked. Fosse's talent was not affected by the drugs, but his behavior became so erratic and energetic that nobody could keep up with him.

It was not well known, but Fosse was an epileptic. So on top of the Dexedrine, he was taking medication for epilepsy. His seizures had always been minor and infrequent until one day during rehearsal at the New Amsterdam Theater. It was a terrible winter and everyone (including Fosse) had the flu. He was on some sort of antibiotic for it, and probably the combination of all three drugs precipitated the attack. We were working with Fosse on stage when suddenly we heard him make this whooping sound, and Gwen Verdon (who had been watching the rehearsal) ran up on stage to catch him as he fell. She cried out to the stage manager, "Call Butterfield 8-1234," which was the phone number of Fosse's psychiatrist. She knew immediately what was happening from the sound. Fosse kept banging his head backward on the stage, and Verdon knelt down and put her knee under his head to protect him. We were all dismissed from the stage, and soon afterward Fosse and Verdon left in a taxi. At that time there was still a prejudice against epilepsy as some form of insanity. What with a grand mal seizure on top of his already hyper behavior, that was probably when the powers-that-be began to think about replacing him.

When the show began previews out of town, the choreography got great reviews, but everything else was in real trouble. Fosse was making revisions to the script right and left and this may have irritated the writer. Fosse also devised an innovative antiwar ballet, done without music. This probably didn't win over the composer. For a big dance number during a political rally, Fosse wrote rhyming words for Truesmith's speech, which sounded like rap before anyone ever heard of rap: "milk, babies, old ladies, hot dogs, puppy dogs" etc. It had every stupid political promise and cliché you've ever heard, and it got a lot of laughs, which probably didn't please the lyricist. It was rumored at the time that some of Fosse's creative partners may have gone to the producers, threatening to withdraw their work if something was not done about Fosse.

It was also rumored that Fosse wanted to take over the leading role. He originally wanted Robert Morse for the part of Truesmith, but David Merrick wouldn't let Morse out of his *Take Me Along* contract. Eddie Bracken (who did the movie), Robert Morse, and Bob Fosse all were short, wiry, and very quick. Tom Poston, who was doing the role, was very heroic-looking but didn't have the same hyper qualities. Fosse would probably have been terrific. In any event, Fosse was fired from his own project—his own show—and it was a real loss to musical comedy.

The Conquering Hero contained some of the most innovative work Fosse ever did. The Okinawa ballet was not only antiwar, but it made a statement about the stupidity of propaganda, and it was truly hilarious. Of course, some people were not amused (a number of ex-Marines walked out) and many people sent telegrams protesting that it was un-American. I think

Fosse was once again ahead of his time. In the ballet the female dancers played the Japanese Army. We carried big knives in our teeth and had bandoliers of bullets crossed over our chests. Our legs below the knee were wrapped as in the old-style Japanese uniforms, and to top it off, we brandished enormous guns. We looked positively ferocious with our caps pulled down over our faces. Most of our dancing was done in deep second-position plié. We acted out every possible cliché about the Land of the Rising Sun. In contrast, the male dancers, playing the U.S. Army, were dressed in gorgeous uniforms and had gold glitter in their hair. They came bounding out of the wings looking incredibly handsome and then stood around in strong-man poses. There was a battle in which the Japanese fared very badly and the Americans emerged victorious. We danced, without music, to the rhythm of the words of Truesmith's mother, as she was talking on the phone explaining to a friend what she thought was going on in the South Pacific. It was a riot.

The opening of the show featured a big parade in which I played the Statue of Liberty. I stood on John Aristede's shoulders. He had a wooden platform hanging around his chest to represent Liberty Island. I knew if I ever fell I would have to jump far enough away from him to clear the "island." John carried me from stage right to stage left, along the downstage edge. I had to keep leaning right and left to dodge different set pieces hanging in the flies near my head. Every night I was terrified I'd fall into the pit. John was holding my ankles; I was holding the torch, the book, and my breath.

Another interesting moment for me came in the amateur talent contest. The winner got to go to the inaugural ball with the mayor's son. My solo was done in toe tap shoes. I hopped all the way to one side of the stage in arabesque to receive a sparkler from the wings and then reversed the hop to the other side to receive a second sparkler. I ended up in the center doing sixteen wings on point making big circles with my arms while holding my wildly sparkling sparklers. (To do a wing, you slide both feet out from the center to the sides and do a shuffle as you bring your feet back together). I'm sure my friends from my days in the Ballet Russe were flabbergasted when they saw me do my toe tap bit, but it was extremely amusing to the rest of the audience.

In the political rally ballet, the dancers were all gathered around the podium listening to Truesmith's rap speech. Every time a word was emphasized, we'd take up the cry and start a different kind of dance to it. Even when he sneezed, we began a Spanish heel dance as we all chanted, "Ah choo, ah choo, ah choo."

The last rehearsal we had with Fosse, we were working on the opening parade. He seemed even more intense than usual, and I said something to

Verdon about it. She said, "Just do whatever he says, Marge. You'll understand later." He worked feverishly to fix the number, and then he said, "Okay, everybody sit down, I've got something to tell you. I've been fired"—you really could have heard a pin drop—"and now I have just a short time left before I have to leave the theater. I don't want anybody to quit, and I want you all to be just as professional and work just as hard for my replacement as you have for me." He then spoke to each of us individually about what we needed to work on to keep growing in our roles. We had all been so excited to be in a new Fosse musical. It was a sad day for everyone in the cast.

That night we had a wake for the show in somebody's hotel room. The entire cast was there, and everyone brought their own bottle. Some serious drinking commenced, as we tried to decipher what had happened and why. In those days, everybody smoked, and the air became a very thick and hazy blue. Finally I'd had enough and, standing up somewhat unsteadily, announced I was leaving. John McMartin offered to walk me home, and I waited near the elevators while he got our coats. The atmosphere was not much better in the hallway than it had been in the room, so I opened the door to the outside fire escape. It was snowing like mad, and the air smelled so fresh and clean that I decided to step out on the platform for a moment. Suddenly I heard the heavy door slam shut behind me. I reached for the doorknob—but there wasn't one. I banged on the door, but no one heard me. There I was, trapped on the sixteenth floor of a hotel in Philadelphia, wearing three-inch heels and a thin dress, in the middle of a blizzard. After what seemed like an eternity, I saw McMartin come out of the hotel onto the sidewalk below. I called to him and after looking to his right and left he finally looked up. A bit astonished he shouted, "What are you doing up there?" "I'm stuck," I answered. "What should I do?" "Well," he said, "why don't you climb down?" I definitely must have had too much to drink because that suggestion made perfect sense to me. How I managed to do it without catching my heels in those metal slats, I'll never know. When I reached the last flight of stairs, which went straight out horizontally, it felt like a gangplank. I walked to the edge, and with much squealing and screeching it finally lowered me to the ground. By this time, of course, quite a little group had gathered. A funny-looking little old lady walked up to me as I stepped off the last stair and said in a quavering voice, "You're not from Philadelphia, are you?!"

Albert Marre and Todd Bolender replaced Fosse as director and choreographer, respectively, but they couldn't make the show work no matter how hard they tried. Then, during one Saturday matinee, after we had opened in New York to horrendous reviews, the word spread that Fosse and Verdon were out front. Even though most of his big numbers were cut, some of Fosse's choreography—for which he was given no credit—was still in the show. The producers were served with an injunction to withdraw the choreography, and the case went to arbitration at Actors Equity. Fosse won the case and established a precedent. The actual amount he won was six cents, which the court tried to give him in change. Fosse insisted on a check, and he got it. Now directors and choreographers receive royalties for their work. They even have their own union called the Society of Stage Directors and Choreographers (SSD&C). When SSD&C was first formed on April 24, 1959, by Agnes De Mille, Shepard Traube, Hanya Holm, Ezra Stone, and Mark Daniels (among others), they had a hard time getting the League of New York Theaters and Producers to acknowledge the union. When Fosse began work on *Little Me*, he refused to start rehearsals until the League officially recognized SSD&C as the collective bargaining agent. They agreed, and on February 14, 1962, the union became a viable operation at last.

One of the things that always made me respect Fosse was that no matter what reversals or bad times he went through in his career, he never gave up. And thank God he didn't. He still had many wonderful shows to create for his appreciative audiences.

How to Succeed in Business Without Really Trying

*T*his megahit musical, a parody of the inefficient workings of big business, definitely made Robert Morse (as the overly ambitious executive) a big star. The show opened on October 14, 1961, and ran four years, for a grand total of 1,417 performances. It won the Pulitzer Prize, the New York Drama Critics Circle Award, and the Tony Award for Best Musical. It also won Tonys for Best Director, Best Actor, Best Lyrics, and Best Libretto. Cy Feuer and Ernest Martin produced it, and Abe Burroughs directed. Burroughs was also one of the writers, along with Jack Weinstock and Willie Gilbert. The wonderful Frank Loesser wrote the music and lyrics. This was to be his last big hit. After this show Loesser did one more musical, *Pleasures and Palaces*, but it never made it into New York. Rudy Vallee starred in *How to Succeed* along with Morse, and the show featured Virginia Martin, Charles Nelson Reilly, and Bonnie Scott.

Burroughs had quite a time directing Bobby Morse. Morse is one of the funniest men in show business, but he is notorious for throwing in all kinds of extraneous stage business—fluttering his hands, doing takes, folding and refolding his arms—until he finally gets around to saying his line. One day Burroughs said to Morse, "Bobby, you know the exit you just made after that scene with Rudy Vallee?" Morse said, "Yeah." "Well," Burroughs said, "get off the stage five minutes earlier."

Although Hugh Lambert was the original choreographer (and he retained the billing), the playbill credited Fosse for the

27

musical staging. Lambert was a choreographer from *The Ed Sullivan Show*, for which he created many good dance numbers. His problem was making numbers work with nondancers. This dilemma is a common one for young choreographers who have worked mostly with dancers. It is much easier to choreograph a number when the bodies you are working with can do anything you dream up. The trick is to make it clever—and make it work—when you have to be dirt-simple. Although there was a regular chorus of dancers in this show, there were also many people who looked like they worked in an office, and they were not dancers—they were singers.

Hugh Lambert got really stuck trying to make the "Paris Original" number work. The producers conferred, and one day after the first few weeks of rehearsal, Fosse and Verdon were simply there. Fosse said he would only come in if Lambert was not let go, because he knew how it felt to be fired. Throughout the rest of the show, Fosse always consulted with Lambert as his assistant. Hugh moved out to the balcony where the dancers he had hired could see his cigarette glowing in the dark. They felt pretty bad for him and would sometimes go up and sit with him when they weren't being used, but they were also falling in love with his replacement. They couldn't believe their luck to be working with Fosse. It was an unusual circumstance for Fosse (he had almost no time for preproduction), but he could work fast when he had to. I'm sure he was working around the clock, with Verdon's assistance. By the time the show opened, Lambert's pirate number (which was terrific) was the only dance of his left in the show. Fosse's numbers were sensational. After the disaster of *Conquering Hero*, it was fortunate that Feuer and Martin believed in Fosse enough to bring him on board.

Donna McKechnie was in the chorus. She was very sick with the flu and felt totally under water during the first few days of rehearsal with Fosse. She felt so terrible she was worried that she'd be fired. She needn't have worried though, as once her natural energy came back they saw what a wonderful dancer she was. She told me she was floored by Fosse's way of working so specifically. She was still pretty new to acting technique, and this was her introduction to the idea of a subtext beneath the movement. After working with Fosse for a while, she began to understand the dialogue he wanted you to have in your mind behind each look or little movement of the hip. He always had a definite point of view or a concept about a number. He was unrelenting in his efforts to articulate what he wanted his performers to express. Dancers had such respect for Fosse that many of them treated him as a father figure. You felt you could really trust this guy. That's probably why he had so many friends.

Fosse was probably more intense than usual on *How to Succeed* because of the *Conquering Hero* fiasco. A lot of pressure was riding on this one for him, and he felt it. One day during rehearsals in the theater, nothing seemed to be going right. He stood up in the house and really bawled out the whole company: called them stupid, and generally gave them hell. The dancers had been trying so hard they just felt mortified. Mara Landi, one of the more outspoken members of the cast, gave it right back to him, and it seemed to calm him down. The same thing had happened in rehearsal for *Redhead*, when Kevin Carlisle stood up to him. I've been told by members of both casts that they almost felt he was trying to get a reaction from someone. Perhaps it served as an outlet for all the tension Fosse felt. In any case, even though he sometimes lost his temper, he almost always gave his dancers showstopping numbers, and they almost always forgave him.

Whenever Fosse shows were out of town, there were many parties where everyone would dance. Elaine Cancilla (for one) told me Fosse always watched carefully how each person expressed himself or herself physically. He loved to catch the essence and humor of each person's movement, and then try to incorporate it into a number. It was like he'd get inside your head to see how you felt when you were dancing, and then he would add his own steps to it. As each dancer did his or her own crazy thing, Fosse shaped, edited, and molded the routine until it was perfect for the moment in the piece.

Three *How to Succeed* numbers—"Coffee Break," "A Secretary is Not a Toy," and "Brotherhood of Man"—were vital to the plot and couldn't be cut. They also had to work. Fosse made sure they did.

The idea behind "Coffee Break" was that people would go mad if there was no coffee when they took their break. To show how upset they were when they arrived at the empty coffee urn, Fosse lined the cast up across the stage and had each one fall backward into the arms of the person behind, creating the look of dominos being knocked over. Everyone went into a more and more frenzied panic. One of the guys (Dale Moreda) even jumped into the pit.

"A Secretary is Not a Toy" was maybe Broadway's first anti–sexual harassment number. The set was a series of office doors across the stage. During the number everyone peeked in and out of the doors, then made many entrances and exits through them. Everyone did many different types of funny walks, with lots of claps and snapping combinations. The tempo kept changing, and people kept exiting and reentering (trying to keep track of where everyone was supposed to be was like trying to win at a shell game). Fosse again used a line of dancers all bending back in a hinge from the knees while holding the person in front around the waist and taking little tiny steps all together.

"Brotherhood of Man" was all about the virtues of being a company man. It started out as a hymn and ended as a rousing spiritual, with each person clapping and stamping like mad, while Ruth Kobart (playing Rudy Vallee's secretary) stood on top of her desk wailing away in the best revivalist manner.

Fosse knew how to use staging details to make a number work. When Fosse worked with Morse on "I Believe in You," he had the terrific idea of using an empty mirror frame above the sink facing the orchestra pit, so the audience could see Morse preening and admiring himself as he sang.

Fosse was also adept at moving smoothly from the end of a scene into the beginning of a number, something Burroughs had difficulty with. Fosse usually wanted the emotion to rise at the end of a scene so the transition to singing would be done seamlessly. Every time Burroughs would get near the end of a scene, he'd look around for Fosse to take over. Sometimes just to tease Burroughs, Fosse would make himself scarce. Fosse admired Burroughs, though, and learned a great deal from him.

Little Me

*A*fter Cy Feuer and Ernest Martin had been clever enough to ask Fosse to do the musical staging for *How to Succeed*, they hired him once again for *Little Me* as choreographer and codirector (with Feuer). *Little Me* starred Sid Caesar and Virginia Martin and opened on Broadway on November 17, 1962. It was based on Patrick Dennis's novel of the same name and adapted for the stage by Neil Simon. The music was by Cy Coleman, the lyrics by Carolyn Leigh.

Now Fosse had two megahits right across the street from each other, *How to Succeed* at the Forty-sixth Street Theater and *Little Me* at the Lunt-Fontanne. This put him back on track after the disastrous *Conquering Hero* and definitely restored people's faith in his talent.

The story is a burlesque of the "as-told-to" biography written by stars of the silver screen, and the show is one of the funniest you could ever see. Virginia Martin played the star, Belle Poitrine, and Sid Caesar played seven of the men in her life, while Swen Swenson played George Musgrove, a childhood sweetheart of Belle's.

The *Little Me* auditions featured a couple of memorable incidents. One day, after Fosse had been auditioning girls for quite a few hours, he had them do a big jump combination across the stage, a combination that ended in a double pirouette. As each girl finished, Fosse would say, "Stay" or "I'm sorry, thank you." One very nervous girl did her preparation and then executed the steps with a frozen smile on her face. When she finished, she turned expectantly toward Fosse; he very nicely said, "Thank you.

I'm sorry." Apparently this was not the reaction she had been expecting. She picked up her large dance bag, walked up to Fosse, who was sitting on a stool at the front of the stage, and hit him so hard with the bag, she knocked him clean off the stool. "Nobody says *I'm sorry* to me!" she screamed. Both stage managers rushed in to take her away. Fosse brushed himself off, smoothed back his hair, and said, "Ladies, no more dance bags on stage."

During this audition period Gwen Verdon, who hadn't been feeling too well, went to her doctor and said, "I don't know what's wrong with me, but test me for everything." A few days later, while Fosse was at the theater and Verdon was at home, her doctor called. He told her she'd better sit down. Expecting to hear the worst, Verdon slowly lowered herself into a chair. "Gwen," the doctor said, "you're pregnant." Verdon let out a yell, hung up the phone, and immediately called Fosse backstage—something she'd ordinarily never do. As soon as she told him the good news, Fosse also let out a yell and dropped the receiver. Fosse ran out in the street and the first person he ran into was Cy Feuer's son, Jed. Verdon thought he had fainted, but he was on Forty-sixth Street shouting, "Gwen is pregnant! Gwen is pregnant! Gwen is pregnant!"

Fosse had produced so many showstopping numbers by this time in his career that people were calling him a genius. I wholeheartedly agree. His talent was incredible, but I also think he was so successful because he did such intensive homework before every show. He was always willing to go that extra mile. If a number didn't work, he had a million other ideas at his fingertips because he had considered every possible interpretation of each musical number beforehand.

There were so many wonderful numbers in *Little Me*, I hardly know where to start, but the first one that comes to mind is "The Rich Kid's Rag." We dancers stood facing each other as couples, with our feet turned in, our knees bent and touching each other, and our backs swayed. We were costumed as very wealthy children would have been around the turn of the century. Fosse told us he got the idea from an old photograph of little girls in low-sashed dresses, rolled knee-high stockings, and long sausage curls. We did the whole dance with the uppity attitude of bratty snobs, our noses in the air. As we prepared to dance with the boys, each girl put one finger on her partner's shoulder and one finger in the palm of his hand. Stylistically it was related to "Uncle Sam's Rag" in *Redhead*. Both numbers used a multitude of different funny walks with many exits and reentrances, once again creating the illusion that there were many more dancers in the number than there really were. ("Rich Kid's Rag" was also a forerunner of "The Rich Man's Frug" still to come in *Sweet Charity*.) Fosse knew how to keep raising the key in the music and changing the tempo in order to build a number in an incredibly exciting way.

In "Deep Down Inside," Belle and the chorus did an energetic hoedown to convince the miserly banker Mr. Pinchley (Sid Caesar) of his inherent goodness. Gretchen Cryer and I had small parts in the scene just before this number, so we couldn't be in it, but this meant we were able to sit out front and watch Fosse rehearse the company. At one point Pinchley appears to be about to strike Belle with his cane. The dancers were told to react to this by putting their hands up in front of their faces, as if to ward off the blow. Fosse said, "Think of those car insurance ads where you see the couple through their windshield, terrified because they're about to have a crash." Cryer and I could see how the subtext Fosse gave to the movement made the performers' feelings crystal clear to the audience. This was one of the many Fosse numbers that had a "clump" in it—a very tight group of people, all doing different gestures (tiny or big), but moving as a unit across the stage. It always has a highly humorous effect—a mobile mass that had arms and legs coming out of everywhere. When *Little Me* was revived twenty years later, Peter Gennaro choreographed the show because Fosse was doing a film. Gennaro was having trouble finding a way to do the hoedown "Deep Down Inside" and asked Fosse if he could come in and do that one number. Fosse did come in and brought with him John Sharpe, who had been the dance captain in *Little Me* and knew every step exactly. When I saw the revival, that number was so good it jumped right off the stage. And recently I saw an old kinescope of "Deep Down Inside" made when we did it on the Ed Sullivan Show. It is a hoedown to end all hoedowns. The audience started clapping way before the number finished and by the end they were cheering like mad.

One day in rehearsal Fosse asked me to work with him and the male dancers on "Dimples," a vaudeville turn for Belle at the point in the show when she is jailed after accidentally shooting Mr. Pinchley. In about an hour he set the entire number, as I played Belle and all the guys played Keystone-type cops. "Dimples" had every vaudeville sight gag you ever heard of. Belle's leotard and tights were striped like a convict's uniform, and she was chased by the cops throughout the entire number. At one point they carried her sideways behind a screen. Another girl was waiting there and her feet were pulled out from one side while Belle's head appeared from the other. It looked like the cops had stretched Belle to be about twelve feet long.

We had just about gotten the number under our belts when Fosse went out of the studio and brought back Neil Simon, Cy Coleman, Carolyn Leigh, Cy Feuer, Ernest Martin, and the entire staff (plus Sid Caesar and Virginia Martin) to see it. I don't know how the fellows felt, but I was quaking in my boots. It looked like the Who's Who of American Musicals sitting there. I guess we didn't do too badly, since "Dimples" was added as a new number for Virginia Martin.

The women had a scene at the end of the first act called "Lafayette We Are Here," in which we played entertainers at a canteen during World War I. Fosse tried everything during the pre-Broadway tour, but he couldn't make this number pay off. Then Fred Werner, who was the dance arranger on the show, remembered a discarded song called "Real Live Girl." All he had was the lead sheet, but he showed it to Gwen Verdon and they started tossing around the idea of having the guys sing it as they waited for the female entertainers to arrive. Werner and Verdon talked to Fosse about it, and he said he would give them one day and one night to work on it. When they came back with some staging and an arrangement, Fosse loved the idea. He decided to give each guy a totally different personality, and the guys would sometimes pretend to be the girls they were all longing to see. It was not only funny but also extremely poignant. At a production meeting Fosse told the staff he was going to slow down the music for a giant soft-shoe section in the middle of the number. Everyone just looked at him blankly as they had no idea what he was talking about, but they finally said, "Great idea!" The first night the song went into the show, it was such a smash that Fosse did a cartwheel in the lobby.

Fred Werner said he felt Fosse really knew how to put a number together. First of all, Fosse was relentless and would never take no for an answer. Also, he was always willing to try every step himself before he made anyone else do it. One time when Fosse was working with Fred Werner, Kathryn Doby, and Louise Quick during preproduction for the film version of *Cabaret*, he wanted to try some sort of back flip. All three of them said, "No, no, don't try it yourself." But Fosse went ahead and did it anyway, falling and cutting his lip. As he stood there holding his jaw with the blood running through his fingers, the first thing he said was, "Don't tell Gwen!"

Another thing Werner felt was unique about Fosse was the way he affected his performers. He made them think they could do much more than they had ever done before. He raised the level of expectation to get the results he wanted.

One of the high points in *Little Me* was Swen Swenson's performance in "I've Got Your Number." I watched every single performance. (Fosse had seen Swenson play the role of Blazes Boylan in *Ulysses in Nighttown* on Broadway in 1958 and he knew this was just the cocky attitude needed for the role of George Musgrove in *Little Me.*) Early on, the song was in danger of being cut from the show, so Fosse began rehearsing with Swenson in the evening after rehearsing all day with the rest of the cast. "I've Got Your

Number" was a striptease—and even though all Swenson took off was his tie, his vest, and his armbands, it was extremely sensuous. As usual Fosse made the sexiness funny, and he kept simplifying and clarifying so that the intention was always laser clear. When he finally had Swenson show the number to the creative team, there was no question the number would stay. It stopped the show cold every single night.

Swenson told me he felt that of all the directors he'd ever worked with, Fosse was the best. He absolutely trusted Fosse to know what would work and what wouldn't. Twenty years later, during the revival of *Little Me*, Swenson called me after the opening and asked, "Did you see my reviews?" Every last critic talked about how great Swen had been in the original "I've Got Your Number."

At the memorial for Bob Fosse, Neil Simon told the following story about the opening night of *Little Me:* He was standing at the back of the house with Cy Coleman and Fosse. He said Sid Caesar, who was otherwise brilliant, coughed on his first three laugh lines, which of course ruined the laughs. Simon looked at Cy Coleman and then they both looked at Fosse. Fosse put his arms down at his sides, closed his eyes, and fell backwards, every part of his body hitting the floor simultaneously. He lay motionless, moaning very quietly. A few minutes later, a very hostile and very inebriated man got out of his seat and walked up the aisle on his way to the men's room. Turning to the three men he said angrily, "This is the worst goddamned show I've seen since *My Fair Lady*." Bob laughed until he cried.

Fosse won a Tony Award for the choreography in *Little Me*, and the show was nominated for six other awards. He just kept getting better and better.

Pleasures and Palaces

*B*ob Fosse was about to embark on his most creative and productive years, but he still had one more trial to go through. *Pleasures and Palaces* was based on a play written by Sam Spewack. Fosse was once again both the director and the choreographer. The show was produced by Allen B. Whitehead in association with Frank Productions Inc. (Frank Loesser's production company). Loesser had seen the Spewack play and decided to turn it into a musical. He composed the score, and he and Spewack rewrote the book. Loesser was one of America's greatest composers. Two of his most wonderful scores were *Guys and Dolls* and *Most Happy Fella,* but this show proved to be a real problem for him.

The four leads were John McMartin, Hy Hazell, Phyllis Newman, and Jack Cassidy (Cassidy replaced Alfred Marks during the pre-Broadway tour). The featured players were Mort Marshall, Leon Janney, Eric Brotherson, Sammy Smith, Woody Romoff, Barbara Sharma, John Anania, and Michael Quinn. Some of the best Fosse dancers were in it. Besides Sharma, he had Kathryn Doby (his assistant), John Sharpe, Eddie Gasper, Leland Palmer, and David Gold, among others. It was a wonderful cast and had equally spectacular people on the creative staff. But somehow, they just couldn't make it work. God knows they tried.

At one point when things were getting desperate, Fosse even considered putting his own money into the show. His marriage to Verdon had produced a lovely daughter named Nicole, who was only a year old at the time. One day Fosse said, in front of the company, "So, the kid doesn't go to Vassar." He really wanted to make that show work.

I was invited to see a run-through before the show went out of town on its pre-Broadway tour. I was expecting at the time, and I was so happy to have the opportunity to see the show. When I arrived at the theater, I was surprised to find I was the only one in the audience. As it turned out, I was about the only one (outside of the cast) who ever did see it, at least in New York.

The story concerned the colorful Catherine the Great (Hy Hazell) and her love interest, Admiral Grigori Potemkin (Jack Cassidy). After the American Revolution, Catherine the Great hired John Paul Jones (John McMartin) to put some fight into the Russian Imperial Navy so they could whip Turkey. John Paul Jones is played as a real bumbling idiot who can do nothing right except win battles. Phyllis Newman played the requisite sexpot (a countess named Sura), who gets involved with both the Admiral and John Paul Jones.

Although the actors did the very best they could with the material, the book was in real trouble, and no one seemed to be able to fix it. The original play, called "Once Upon a Russian," had bombed in New York and closed in two days. The critics in Detroit didn't like the book of the musical any better, or the score for that matter. They said Loesser's music had few bright moments and Spewack's story line didn't make you care very much about what happened to anybody. On the other hand, the sets by Robert Randolph and the costumes by Freddy Wittop were gorgeous. The Turkish scene that opened the second act always got a hand.

However, the reviews did say the dancing was charming, and the critics especially loved a cooch number (which I also adored) called "The Turkish Delight," featuring Barbara Sharma, with four other girls. They said Sharma's sexy, funny belly dance was truly memorable, and her exuberant undulations a bright spot in the show. It even made one critic want to bill and coo. The critics also enjoyed Phyllis Newman's interpretation, and said she was "delightfully rotten to the core."

Other numbers also worked beautifully. "Bara Banchik" was particularly impressive. It started on a black, bare stage with a stamping sound audible offstage. The lights came up as all the dancers marched on. The women took positions as guards, while the men did a takeoff on a wild Russian character dance reminiscent of the Moiseyev. There were many solo turns, each man competing to see who could do the most difficult steps. Fosse loved to have men dance in a very strong, masculine way.

Fred Werner, the musical director, told me about one number with Phyllis Newman and Jack Cassidy that was added on the road. It was supposed to be very Scheherazade-like and romantic, as the man serenades his lady while they gallop on horseback across a desert. Here's what *really* happened. A mechanical horse was pulled out on stage, a long extension cord visible behind it. Cassidy turned on the switch and Newman (who was on the horse) started going up and down, as if she were on a ride at an amusement park. They couldn't both fit on the horse, so Cassidy just stood next to her and sang this serious love song, "You Are My Thunder and Lightning." Fred said that it was unintentionally hilarious. Fosse kept saying he was sure he could fix it if he just had a little more time.

Loesser acted like the show's failure didn't bother him very much, and whenever he was asked a question he would say, "Fine, fine." However, I'm sure he was heartbroken that the show wasn't working. The cast said he always carried around lots of bags of candy for them, but very often when he was needed, he could not be found.

Johnny Sharpe (a wonderful performer) spent a lot of time rehearsing the dancers in the lobby, while Fosse was on stage with the principals trying to find the changes that would make it work. Cassidy and Newman were playing their parts for comedy, and McMartin was as engaging as only he can be, but Hy Hazell was a serious actress from London. They all were coming from very different backgrounds, and no one could ever agree on what kind of show they wanted to be doing. One critic said the show couldn't make up its mind whether to be an old-fashioned costume melodrama or a commentary on current Russian–American relations.

The dancers absolutely adored Fosse, and worked as hard as they could for him. When he finally had to tell them they were closing, many of them cried. At their last rehearsal, he said he thought he had figured out a way to solve the number "Tears of Joy." Fosse had changed this number many times. First he cut the lyrics, but eventually he even cut the music, reducing the number to rhythms, claps, stamps, and a few accented words. Although it had started as a serious dance, he now wanted to add his famous humor to it. He asked if the dancers would mind working on it for him, even though it would never be seen because they were closing, and according to the union they didn't have to rehearse. Of course they all agreed to do it. When he was finished, the number worked splendidly, but there was no money left to do the orchestrations and no time left to get it into the show. They were closing in two days. The cast even offered to pay for the orchestrations, but the time frame made it quite impossible. (It is almost unheard of for dancers to put their own money behind their belief in a director.) After the final rehearsal was over, the cast wanted to cheer him up; they spontaneously started doing numbers from his other shows. This time it was Fosse's turn to get teary-eyed.

Alice Evans and Barbara Sharma both said Fosse really was interested in the development of his people. He wanted to bring out a particular personality, not just fit a dancer into a mold. He could also be very caring. When Alice Evans auditioned to understudy the Catherine the Great part, she told Bobby—with much trepidation—that she had some burn scars on one arm. She was almost sure she had the understudy, but she was worried that her scars would show. Fosse asked her to come on stage in her slip under the lights. Afterwards, he came backstage and said with a smile, "I don't see any scars." She got the job.

Barbara Sharma once asked him for some career advice. She couldn't decide whether or not she should go out to the West Coast. She had been asked to replace the lead in the television series *Gidget*. Fosse said she should go. She didn't take his advice. Instead she stayed in New York so she could work with him. She was a featured dancer in three of his shows but it wasn't the prestige of a lead in a television series. Barbara said that often after rehearsal with Fosse she would be so tired, she couldn't wait to get home and just soak her feet. Many times she would wake up only to realize it was already morning, and she was sitting there fully clothed with her feet in ice-cold water. Ah, the glamour of show business!

Sweet Charity

I really loved *Sweet Charity*. When I saw it, shortly after the opening, I couldn't stop crying. I was crying not only because I wasn't in it (I'd recently given birth to my daughter Pamela and was literally out of shape) but also because I saw Fosse's talent simply exploding all over the stage.

Sweet Charity, conceived by Fosse, based on Federico Fellini's movie *The Nights of Cabiria*, and directed and choreographed by Fosse, opened at the Palace Theater on January 29, 1966, and ran for 608 performances. The show starred Gwen Verdon in the title role, and John McMartin played Oscar, the man who almost marries Charity. Helen Gallagher and Thelma Oliver were her two sidekicks (Nickie and Helene), and James Luisi played the movie star (Vittorio Vidal). Cy Coleman wrote the music, and the lyrics were by Dorothy Fields. The show won all kinds of awards, including a Tony for the choreography for Fosse.

Fosse wrote the original script of *Sweet Charity* as a one-act musical, under the pen name Bert Lewis (his full name was Ro*bert Louis* Fosse). His idea was to do an evening of three unrelated one-acts. The other two scripts, which were written by other people, were problematic, however. In one of them, Verdon played a cat burglar and would have had to wear suction cups on her hands and feet and crawl straight up a wall. It was extremely dangerous. Eventually the producers decided to expand the *Charity* script to a full-length show.

Fosse worked on the script for quite some time, but he finally decided to ask Neil Simon to collaborate with him on it. Simon—who loved it—said he would. (Simon's remarkable track record of hits also made it easier to raise the money needed for the show.) Simon added some jokes and some terrific story ideas, but it was still basically Fosse's script.

I saw the show at the newly renovated Palace Theater. On the outside, everything at the Palace looked so beautiful and new, but all was not so rosy underneath. The Palace was built in 1913 and *Sweet Charity* opened early in 1966. As far as I've been able to discover, the 1965 renovation was the first. The trouble was, a lot of it was cosmetic; nobody worried too much about what was under the pretty paint.

There was no air conditioning; the management's idea of a cooling system consisted of a fan blowing over a block of ice. In the middle of one New York heat wave that summer, Verdon put a thermometer in her coat pocket when they were up in the parachute scene. It read 108 degrees. Everyone was complaining about the heat, but they were told it was just unfortunate weather.

In another unfortunate incident a worker accidentally broke into a sewer line, and there was waste floating all over the basement. When the cast complained to Actors Equity, the union suggested the producers buy the performers galoshes. Verdon told me they had rats backstage as big as cats. Between the heat and the fumes, performers were dropping like flies. The cast kept complaining to the union to force the theater to do something about it, but to no avail. Finally Verdon got an attorney and sued Equity for nonrepresentation. At last Equity backed up the performers and, between the producers and the theater management, almost everything got fixed. It must have been the performers' loyalty to Fosse that kept them all from quitting.

But back to the show. "The Rich Man's Frug" (which is part of the night-club scene) started with Fosse's favorite type of dance—a trio. The three terrific dancers in the Broadway production were Eddie Gasper, Barbara Sharma, and John Sharpe. They started with tight, sexy little moves with an underlying cynical humor to them. The men walked leaning forward in sway-backed position toward Sharma, who was floating her arms about her wriggling hips. Then the number expanded to include the chorus. Each one held a lit cigarette (in a long holder) to his mouth with one hand, keeping his other hand on his vest pocket. (When he had to get rid of his lit cigarette he shoved it into his vest pocket, which was lined with asbestos.) As the men moved, they waggled their heads back and forth with a supercilious air. The women walked leaning way back in a hinge—their bodies in a straight line from the shoulders to the hips and their arms hanging straight down behind them. They had the cool and elegant air of the very rich. The number was in four sections: The Frug, The Aloof, The Heavyweight, and The Big Finish. Each section started with a basic theme. Then variations were introduced, building with such intensity you wondered where the dancers found the strength. During early rehearsals for this number at Variety Arts Studios, a major blackout occurred in most of Manhattan. Fosse thought it was only a blown fuse in the building he was in, so he gathered all the flashlights and candles he could find and continued working. His concentration and focus were not going to be disturbed, no matter what was going on in the outside world.

"If My Friends Could See Me Now" was a tour de force for Verdon. Each step was a polished gem. Its spot in the show is the scene in which the movie star (who has picked her up) gives her mementos of their evening together. One of them is a pop-open top hat. Fosse's inventiveness with where and how he had Verdon pop that hat never quit. As the movie star gave her each new souvenir, Charity danced in a very sassy way, looking like the cat that swallowed the canary. She had the glee and happiness that only a poor dance hall girl could feel at this unbelievable event, being wooed by a big star. Nobody has ever done Fosse's choreography better than Verdon did—or expressed his intent as well.

Charity and her two cohorts, Nickie and Helene, do a song called "There's Gotta Be Something Better Than This," which was another stunner. Very seldom have I seen a female dance number with such power to it. Each girl had her own section in which she expressed her dissatisfaction with her present circumstances and explained how she planned to better her future. As each one began to believe she might be able to do something about her life, that there were other possibilities, she became more and more excited and elated. The number built to an exuberant dance for the three of them and ended with a roaring finish. The hard part was the ending; when they were totally out of breath, they had to sing again, holding those last notes seemingly forever.

Gene Foote, a dancer in the show, said Fosse loved to make each movement a character study rather than only a dance step. One of the funniest steps in "Rhythm Of Life" had its genesis with a little old man Fosse saw running after a bus. Foote also told me this wonderful belief that Fosse lived by: "The time to sing is when your emotional level is too high to just speak anymore, and the time to dance is when your emotions are just too strong to only sing about how you feel."

One of the most hysterical scenes in the show was based on an incident that actually happened during the pre-Broadway tour. Joan Simon (Neil Simon's wife) told this to Gwen Verdon. Neil Simon had been having trouble writing a scene about group therapy, and he was trying to find another situation to take its place. One day Mr. and Mrs. Simon were leaving for the theater when they got stuck in the elevator of the Jefferson Hotel. Neil has claustrophobia, and he was going crazy waiting for someone to get them out. Joan tried to calm him down by playing trivia games with him, but Neil just kept getting more and more agitated, and he started sweating like mad. Joan would ask him a trivia question and Neil would nervously answer as he first took off his coat and then started fanning himself with his hat. He still couldn't cool down so he removed his jacket and finally his tie. When they were rescued at last, the door opened and they burst out of the elevator onto the lobby floor. Neil, who was ashen by this time, said to Joan, *"I have to get back in!"* Joan looked at him in disbelief and asked, *"Why?"* Neil told her he had to go back up to their room to write the scene they had just lived through. Which he did. This became the very funny elevator scene with Verdon and McMartin.

I got to do a four-month summer tour of *Sweet Charity* two years later, playing Nickie and understudying Charity. Paul Glover, who had been in the Broadway production, restaged the original choreography. He had also assisted Fosse with the national tour, the London tour, and the film. Glover knew that show like the back of his hand and was so meticulous about recreating every nuance that it was almost like doing it for Fosse himself.

Glover described the endings to the show Fosse had used, which had been different for each production, and asked me which one I thought would be the best. I told him I had no idea. That night the most unusual thing happened. I had a dream in which I saw Charity after she's pushed into the lake near the end of the show. In my dream she pulled herself back up on the stage and while she was wringing herself out and emptying her shoes of water, she said to the audience, "Did you ever have one of those days?" The music came sneaking back in underneath as she went to pick up her suitcase and plant, and slowly she began to sing some of Dorothy Field's lyrics as she walked to the center of the stage. Then I woke up. I knew the lyrics were from the song "Bravest Individual." I ran into the other room to find my music, and the lyrics jumped out at me:

> So when I panic and feel each day
> I've come to the end of the line,
> then I say, that fear hasn't licked me yet
> and I say to myself,
> "I'm the bravest individual I have ever met."

In my dream Charity sang the first two lines as she walked toward center stage; the third and fourth lines she sang from center stage. Then as she walked upstage the orchestra played the melody to the final line. She then turned back to face the audience and, as the final melody was repeated, she sang the last phrase, backing away from the audience on the last few syllables. Finally she moved into the opening pose while the black backdrop opened up behind her to reveal a triangle of blazing crimson-red. So that's the ending we used. Much to everyone's satisfaction, it really worked. When Paul told Fosse about it he said, "That's it. That's the ending I was trying to find." I was amazed.

Recently Verdon told me about another ending to the show that I had never heard about. It also would have been better than the one they used on Broadway. In this ending, after Charity pulled herself out of the lake and started to dry herself off, a hot dog and souvenir vendor came along and gave her a balloon. She then decided to write a note, and as she was writing it, she said the words out loud, "Whoever you are and wherever you are, I love you." She then tied the note to the balloon and released it up to the sky.

"Big Spender" was an incredible number to perform. It started with all the girls, their backs to the audience, in a line across the stage. We were playing very bored and weary dance hall girls. Facing upstage, we slowly walked backward toward the audience. Our hands were on our aching backs, our feet were rolling over at the ankles, and our hips shifted from side to side with each step. There was a railing downstage that stretched almost the entire width of the stage. It came out of the floor on four pneumatic pistons that made a wonderful hissing sound as it rose. When we arrived downstage, we suddenly turned toward the audience, and hanging onto or leaning over the railing, each of us fell into a different dead-eyed but seductive pose. It was so effective that every night the orchestra had to keep vamping until the audience stopped laughing and applauding—and we hadn't even *started* the body of the number yet! Glover told us that Fosse wanted absolutely no expression on our faces; we were moving in a very hot, sensuous way, but our faces were completely cold. As we sang the song, the movements alternated between very tight precision and raucous improvisation before we fell into another exhausted-looking pose. The steps clearly expressed the girls' attempts to entice the men who were looking on and deciding who they wanted for a partner. Each time we got to the musical interlude after singing the line "Hey, big spender!" the stage would suddenly erupt with explosive movement and just as suddenly go back to complete stillness. The choreography reminded me of a Picasso line drawing: Fosse took away all the frills and left only what was essential to express—powerfully—an emotional idea.

When the tour ended, I was never so sad to see a show close. I thought I'd never do another musical I loved as much—and now, so many years later,

I still feel the same way. This show marked the beginning of Fosse's most creative period.

I'm glad we have Fosse's films and videos available for students to study. His dances always had a reason for being, and he knew how to build a number as very few ever have: with imaginative, dynamic movement, humor, key and tempo changes, meaningful subtext, and plenty of sex.

When the movie of *Sweet Charity* was released the reviews were not good, but Fosse was, as usual, way ahead of his time. His many fast cuts were very foreign to our eyes then, but now the film looks as though it had been made yesterday. Verdon taught Shirley MacLaine all the dances for the movie version, and got MacLaine to move perfectly in the Fosse style. If you've never seen the movie version of *Sweet Charity*, rent it. It's required research for any lover of dance, and a great film besides.

Pippin

*I*n 1972 Fosse won a Tony Award for choreographing and directing the show *Pippin*. He won an Emmy for the television special *Liza with a Z*, and he also won the Oscar for the film *Cabaret*. He became the only person, before or since, to win three awards in three different fields of show business for work done in the same year. It was an incredible feat. People were calling him the King of Showbiz.

He also did one of those television and print ads for American Express. It began "You may not know my name but . . . ." In the picture he was positively beaming. He looked happier than I'd ever seen him. He really was a winner, and at last he seemed to know it.

Before all this success, during rehearsals for *Pippin*, John Mineo told me that Fosse was very bitter and down about the failure of the film *Sweet Charity*. It had been six years since his last Broadway musical. Even though his use of drugs was probably at its height, he was still able to be extremely creative. He wanted to put all his sexual fantasies on the stage. Nine years later, when he started work on a television version of *Pippin*, he came at the show from a totally different place, and it had a much sweeter feel. Fosse's life always influenced what he put on the stage. For the television version Fosse used twelve cameras and taped three performances with live audiences. He also had two days' worth of doing inserts. Unfortunately Bob was unable to come to terms with the producers. He never edited the tapes and we never got the chance to see the final product as he envisioned it.

Pippin was produced on Broadway by Stuart Ostrow and written by Roger O. Hirson. It opened on November 23, 1972. The action was set in 780 A.D., during the reign of the Holy Roman Empire (or thereabouts, as it said in the program). The music and lyrics were by Stephen Schwartz. According to people in the show, Fosse and Schwartz had very different viewpoints on just about everything. This experience may have influenced Fosse (on *Dancin'* and *Big Deal)* to almost exclusive use of composers who weren't around anymore. John Rubinstein played Pippin, Jill Clayburgh played Catherine (Pippin's love interest), Leland Palmer played Fastrada (the king's second wife), Eric Berry played the King, Shane Nickerson played the little boy, Irene Ryan was her usual terrific self as the grandmother, and Ben Vereen leaped to stardom as the Leading Player.

Kathryn Doby and Louise Quick were Fosse's assistants. The ten incredible original dancers were Ann Reinking, Candy Brown, Kathryn Doby, Pamela Sousa, Jennifer Nairn-Smith, John Mineo, Dick Korthaze, Gene Foote, Chris Chadman, and Paul Solen. Doby said Fosse made each dancer feel he or she had a definite character and was as important to the show as the leads. (This was before Michael Bennett did *A Chorus Line,* so it was highly unusual for the dancers to be considered interesting as individuals.)

The show got mixed reviews, and for a while it didn't look like it was going to last. Then Fosse made the first-ever television commercial for a Broadway show, and it turned out brilliantly. In it, he used many of the new techniques he had learned as a film director. The commercial boosted sales and caused the show to catch on and have a five-year run.

Ann Reinking first met Fosse at the audition for *Pippin.* She was dismayed when she saw the huge number of people who showed up, but after a while she became so intrigued by the work, she forgot it was even an audition. She said the combinations Fosse gave them were not only good, but also unique. They included wonderful pantomime and at the same time, they were moving or isolating some parts of the body while other parts remained totally still.

She told me he was able to spin a web that made her feel secure, relaxed, and as if she were sharing in the creative experience. When he made his dancers feel that trusted, it somehow instilled in them the drive and desire to be really good, and made them want to give their all.

Fosse usually did not ask dancers to do anything he couldn't do, but once he started working more closely with Reinking, he began to stretch as a choreographer beyond anything he himself could do as a dancer. Her technique and strength were so marvelous, Fosse knew she could do whatever he could think up. Fosse learned from all the important women in his life. Joan

McCracken taught him all about classical music, and Verdon taught him . . . everything else.

He pulled a practical joke on Reinking when the show was playing at the Kennedy Center in Washington during the pre-Broadway tour. She was up on the roof of the theater with Fosse and Leland Palmer and a couple of other dancers, looking out over the city. Fosse told her his dancers were so devoted to him that if he told them to jump off the roof, they would do it immediately and without question. Ann said, "Oh, sure!" Fosse said to the other dancers, "Jump!" and they did jump right off the roof. Ann almost fainted with fright. Of course, it had all been planned beforehand, and there was a landing just below that she couldn't see.

In *Pippin*, as in all his shows, Fosse's use of lighting transformed the movement. Jules Fisher was the lighting designer, and the two men worked together beautifully. For "Magic To Do," the opening number, Fisher constructed a trough full of lights covered by a grating that went across the whole stage. The lights shot straight up from the floor to make a curtain of light. The cast wore black robes with hoods that hid their faces. They stood just upstage of the light, and while they sang, they gestured in the light with their white-gloved hands to express the meaning of the words. (One gesture was to wipe the blood off their hands.) Only Ben Vereen's face could be seen. It looked like his head and all the hands were floating in the air. The movements were small, but very precise, and each one was crystal clear.

Fisher's lighting directed the audience's attention to wherever Fosse chose for them to look. At one point Ben Vereen pointed with his cane to a small red kerchief lying on the stage. A bright spotlight moved away from Ben and landed on it. Then Ben bent down and gestured for the kerchief to rise; little by little, it rose straight up to reveal that it was attached to macrame ropes in intricate designs, which spread higher and wider until they curtained the whole stage all the way up to the proscenium arch. The effect was wondrous and magical. Of course nowadays, with helicopters landing and chandeliers crashing on the stage, this may not seem so spectacular, but at that time it was very innovative.

The show is about a young prince (Pippin) who is trying to find himself. He first becomes a revolutionary and rebels against his father, the king. Then he assassinates the king and takes his place. He eventually becomes a warmonger, which triggers the "War is a Science" number. The entire cast sat on a long bench downstage and performed a minstrel show. Everyone wore white gloves and clapped and stamped out a number of syncopated rhythms, even using tambourines at one point. Then the Leading Player sings "Glory" to Pippin, telling him how great war will make him feel. In the middle of the number, Pam Sousa and Candy Brown entered with canes and straw hats and joined Vereen in the famous trio dance (this is the dance used in the television commercial). The cast nicknamed it The Manson Trio, because three different murders were staged behind it. Dick Korthaze was killed in the first segment, Paul Solen in the second, and Ann Reinking in the third. There is an eventual battle; heads and limbs are thrown all over the place, and during one sequence, the number of people who have died in each war is read over the loudspeakers as the cast looks at the audience with cruel amusement. When the battle ends, Pippin is alone on the stage with all the dead bodies. This is sickening to him, and glory and gore become his first disappointment.

The leading player lures him into the next scene, simply called "The Flesh." This was one of the sexiest numbers ever done in a Broadway show. One at a time the girls entice Pippin and play with him. (Pippin is like a boy in a candy store.) Finally, two girls sandwich Pippin between themselves. One of the girls takes his hand and puts it on her bust. Pippin looks straight out front and, with a big grin on his face, says, "I found it!" After a calypso section, through a big keyhole two girls can be seen caressing each other. Then the girls lead Pippin to an opium den and bring him his very own pipe. As Pippin gets high, the boys run in; grabbing his arms and legs, they lift him up in the air spread-eagled. Each time they lower his body, another girl rolls underneath him. Finally satiated, Pippin climbs up the proscenium arch to get away from them. Everyone climbs after him, clawing at him, and he finally cries out, "Enough! Let me alone!" The joys of the flesh have also begun to pale.

Then Pippin tries politics, but through circumstances and events the Leading Player points out how crooked politics are and Pippin gets disappointed in that too.

Pippin finally tries to find peace on a farm as a husband and father. Fosse showed the consummation of Pippin's affair with the woman who owns the farm in a unique way. As they climb into bed the lights fade out on them and come up on two dancers entering from opposite sides of the stage (Gene Foote and Kathryn Doby). They are wearing very skimpy, erotic costumes. They both show how excited they are by wiggling up and down and rubbing their hands all over their bodies and heads in a frenzy of excitement. (Gene Foote was a riot doing this.) An insistent bolero is playing, and the two dancers beat their heels frantically into the floor. The orchestration builds to a grand climax as the two dancers run toward each other for the big lift. They miss each other and fall in a heap just as the lights black out on them and come up on the bed. Pippin lifts his head, groans and says, "I'm sorry!" Then the lights fade out on them as the two dancers enter once more. This time the lift ends successfully and when the audience once again sees Pippin and his lady in their bed, they are all smiles. It was hysterical. Doby was not able to do that particular section on opening night because she had stamped her heels so hard in rehearsal, she'd gotten terrible shinsplints and couldn't do the step. Fosse seemed to have that affect on people.

(If you will forgive my digression, it reminds me of a rehearsal I once had with Fosse. We were doing an excerpt from *Pal Joey* at a special performance at the City Center Theater. We were rehearsing this strong scootch step with a contraction while we moved forward in one direction and at the same time looked back where we had come from. I was dancing so strongly and trying so hard to impress Fosse, that I crashed my knee right into a radiator.)

As time goes by, Pippin even becomes dissatisfied with the idyllic pastoral situation. He has become disillusioned with everything. Ultimately, the players try to get Pippin to commit suicide by burning himself up. The subtext Fosse gave the players was that Pippin had to die in order for them to be satisfied lasciviously, and he let the dancers choose and express their own sexual preference improvisationally.

Gene Foote found *Pippin* to be Fosse's most exacting show. There was so much to do and think about during each moment that he felt he was never able to express everything Fosse wanted in any single performance. Foote said he felt Fosse's showstopping ability came from his knowledge of how to build a number to a climax—to give it a beginning, a middle, and an end—and his ability to do it with humor.

When I first saw the show, I was struck by the similarities between Fosse's life and Pippin's. Although Fosse was never involved in politics, he had definite ideas about how our government should be run, and he was certainly an authority figure. I'm sure he must have felt the strain of being the popular, and then sometimes the unpopular, decision-maker. He also tried, at different times in his life, being the playboy, the husband, and the father, with varied success. In the script Pippin says, "Nothing ever turns out the way I planned. I can't do the same thing day and night. I want my life to mean something." And in a moment near the end of the musical, he states, "You have to be dead to find out if you were any good."

I wrote a fan letter to Fosse after seeing *Pippin*, in which I told him that I loved every moment of it. I also told him I'd been to a party afterwards, where I'd seen Stan Lebowsky, the musical director. I'd told Stan the show reminded me of Fosse's life, and Stan said, "You must know him pretty well, because just before the opening Bob said to the cast, 'Well, if they don't like it, they don't like me, 'cause it's the story of my life.'" I received a note back

PLATE 1: *Bob Fosse, arms outstretched to evoke something from the cast.*

PLATE 2:
Carol Haney seductively dancing in the comic "Jealousy Ballet," from Pajama Game.

PLATE 3: *Trio in "Steam Heat," from* Pajama Game. *Hips and shoulders forward with feet turned in, Fosse style. From left to right: Michael Gallagher, Margery Beddow, and Eddie Dudek.*

PLATE 4: *Margery Beddow in "Whatever Lola Wants," from* Damn Yankees, *doing the stalking step toward her assigned prey, baseball player Joe Hardy.*

PLATE 6: *Gwen Verdon and Eddie Phillips in "Who's Got the Pain When They Do the Mambo?" from* Damn Yankees.

PLATE 5: *Harvey Evans (Hohnecker) looking about twelve years old as one of the baseball players in* Damn Yankees.

PLATE 7: *Gwen Verdon and John Aristedes in the very sexy "Whore House Ballet," from* New Girl in Town.

PLATE 8: *Top photo: In foreground, Buzz Miller and Gwen Verdon doing "Pickpocket Tango," in which she manages to steal the keys from the guard in* Redhead. *Behind the bars are all the ladies in the ensemble. This is the jail set that fell on Gwen's feet during the out-of-town tryout.*

PLATE 9: *Bottom photo: Gwen Verdon rehearsing for the military dance section of "Essie's Vision," in* Redhead.

PLATE 10: *Trio doing the famous Fosse scootch step in "At the Check Apron Ball," from* New Girl in Town. *From left to right: Harvey Evans (Hohnecker), Gwen Verdon, and Harvey Jung.*

PLATE 11: *Bob Fosse rehearsing the "War Ballet," from* The Conquering Hero, *which he danced to without music.*

PLATE 12: *Drum majorettes from left to right: Margery Beddow, Jane Mason, and Patricia Ferrier Kiley in the opening "Parade" number, from* The Conquering Hero.

PLATE 13: *The company singing "Coffee Break," from* How to Succeed in Business Without Really Trying. *Charles Nelson Reilly is leaning on coffee cart. The fervor Fosse can elicit from his singers and dancers is clear in this shot.*

PLATE 14: *The extraordinary Swen Swenson dancing "I've Got Your Number," from* Little Me. *He unfailingly stopped the show doing this number.*

PLATE 15: *Bob Fosse, center, showing the men the style and line of a step in* Pleasures and Palaces.

PLATE 16: *Barbara Sharma in foreground as the wildly comic harem girl in "Turkish Delight," from* Pleasures and Palaces.

PLATE 17: *Group dancing in the Heavyweight Section of "Rich Man's Frug," from* Sweet Charity. *Fosse's humorous way of showing the war between the sexes.*

PLATE 18: *Group dancing in the explosive part of "Hey, Big Spender," from* Sweet Charity. *Carmen Hilton and Margery Beddow in the foreground.*

PLATE 19: *Carmen Hilton and Margery Beddow singing "Baby Dream Your Dream," from* Sweet Charity.

PLATE 20: *Top photo: group dancing in the Flesh Section of "Sex Presented Pastorally," from* Pippin. *Cameron Smith center.*

PLATE 21: *Bottom photo: this trio dance, part of the War Section from* Pippin, *was used in the famous commercial for the show. Left to right: Nancy Miller, Thomas Young, and Louise Quick.*

PLATE 22: *Fred Mann III and Barbara Yaeger in "Joint Endeavor," from* Dancin'.

PLATE 23: *Bob Fosse concentrating on the score during rehearsal.*

from Fosse thanking me for my letter, but he denied that the show was the story of his life. He said, and I quote, "That starts tomorrow." Hmmmm. Actually, I guess he wasn't kidding, because after *Pippin* he immediately began one of his most creative periods, starting with the television special *Liza with a Z* and moving on to the magnificent film *Cabaret.*

Chicago

C *hicago* opened at the Forty-sixth Street Theater on June 5, 1975 and ran for two years. I was thrilled to death but also scared to pieces when I auditioned to be Gwen Verdon's understudy. It had been years since I worked directly with Fosse. He was very patient and really took his time with me. I was there for forty-five minutes. He even had the pianist, Johnny Morse, teach me part of one of Verdon's songs, "Funny Honey." I shook like a leaf as I sang and danced for him, but I got a call back.

A short time later, Fosse assembled his cast (minus the as-yet-not-decided-on understudies) and went into rehearsal. One day during the first week, Fosse suddenly began to feel very sick. He was rushed to the hospital, and the prognosis was not good. He arrived in the nick of time, because he'd been about to have a heart attack. His doctor told him he needed surgery to replace an artery in his heart that was badly damaged. Gwen Verdon told the cast what had happened, and it helped that she was the one to talk to them, but everyone was devastated.

The producers, Robert Fryer and James Cresson, decided not to give up on doing the show, but to postpone it until Fosse could continue. They tried to keep the cast together by getting them other work until they knew if, or when, they could start up again. John Kander and Fred Ebb (who wrote the music and lyrics) even wrote a new cabaret act for Chita Rivera. She was one of the three stars contracted for the show. The other two were Gwen Verdon and Jerry Orbach. (Audiences who know Jerry Orbach as an actor from his movies and the *Law and Order* television series may be surprised to know he has been very successful as a leading man in many musicals. He got his start as the original El Gallo in *The Fantasticks*.) It was an incredible cast, from the three stars to the featured players (Barney Martin, Mary McCarty, and M. O'Haughey) down to each member of the ensemble. Fosse again had Kathryn Doby as his assistant, and Tony Stevens was the assistant choreographer.

Everyone held their breath for a few months, and then when Fosse was only partially recovered, they decided it was time to bring everyone back together. Three days before rehearsals were to begin, I finally had my call back. I thought maybe I had a chance ... but I didn't get it. Ah well, that, my dears, is show business.

I saw Fosse up at Broadway Arts Studios shortly after rehearsals began, and gave him a tiny hug. I was truly afraid to touch him. Open-heart surgery was still pretty rare then and it seemed like a miracle that he was back and working.

Four years later, *All That Jazz* was released. This film was maybe his most brilliant work, and it centered around his very real brush with death. Roy Scheider did such an amazing job of portraying Fosse that everyone who knew Fosse had to keep rubbing their eyes to make sure it wasn't him. The scene in the operating room, of actual open-heart surgery, was terrifying to watch, but oh my God, what a great film. Every time I see it, I see more in it than I did the time before.

Fosse and Fred Ebb wrote the book for *Chicago*. More and more Fosse was doing the writing on his projects, and he was finally getting recognition for it. He got full author credit for the films *Lenny* and *Star 80*, and for the Broadway show *Big Deal*.

Anyway, *Chicago* takes place in the Roaring Twenties. For forty-seven years, no woman in Chicago had ever received the death penalty for killing her man. As a matter of fact, in many cases after the woman got off, she went on to become a star in vaudeville. To play in vaudeville had always been a dream of Roxie Hart's (Gwen Verdon), but instead of becoming a star, she got married to a garage mechanic. As she becomes bored with her lot, she begins an affair with the guy who sold them their furniture—Fred.

Graciela Daniele, who was one of the original dancers in *Chicago*, told me about rehearsing the show. Daniele was beginning to work as a choreographer herself then and had almost stopped performing when Fosse asked her to be part of the show. She was in such awe of him and had so much respect for him that she immediately agreed. She wanted to watch him from close up, to understand how he worked. The thing she couldn't get over was his ability not only as a choreographer, but also as a director. He taught the dancers how to be so clear in their intention and organic to the character that they got an almost magical feeling of being able to communicate clearly any state of mind or emotion. She said he really knew how to bring out the best work in each performer. The first day everyone was very nervous (as is always the case). The dancers rehearsed alone with Fosse for a week before anyone else came in. Bob spent the first hour or so showing them pictures of dances from that era (like the black bottom) and then doing bits of movement to get them into the style and period. Graciela said it was like being with a master painter as he starts to sketch. As they began to get the feeling for it, he told them to go to the corner of the rehearsal room and open a trunk that was sitting there. He had each dancer pick a prop from the trunk to build his or her character around. Of course, there was a lot of good-natured laughter, and arguments about who would get which hat, scarf, cane, or boa, but eventually it all got sorted out.

They began by working on the memorable opening number, "All That Jazz," which featured the fantastic Chita Rivera and all the dancers. Chita had one of the best entrances I've ever seen. The orchestra was on top of a very high, round platform upstage center. It looked like an enormous drum. After the overture, while the orchestra did that famous suspenseful vamp, two doors slid open on the side of the drum underneath the band. The inside was filled with blazing light. Then Chita rose up out of the middle of the floor on an elevator. Her movement was tiny, but very intense and suggestive. Near the end of the number, the dancers made their separate entrances climbing down the sides of the bandstand. They each improvised within their own very well-defined character.

Gene Foote said Fosse told them to feel like they were the living dead and to dare the audience to watch them. At one point in the music all these different characters who had been doing their own type of moves suddenly turned front and started to dance in unison. All at once the number froze, and the drum opened once again to reveal in a pool of light, Roxie (Gwen Verdon) and her lover (Chris Chadman) in bed. They rolled once to the right and once to the left. Then the man sat up and began to put on his socks and his pants. He stood up and began to tell Roxie he was leaving her. Roxie said to him sweetly, "Oh, Fred . . . ." Drawing a gun, she yelled at him, *Nobody walks out on me!* and abruptly put three bullets into him. Then she said in a small voice, "Ooooh, I have to pee." There was an immediate blackout on them, and then Fosse had the lights come back up on Chita and the group as he continued to build the number. Like a master carpenter he overlapped different themes, edging up the keys, and goosing the tempo as well as the volume, until he brought the number to a splendid finish.

After the New York run the show went on the road to play the Civic Light Opera in Los Angeles, which was being run at that time by Feuer and

Martin. The board was known for being rather straitlaced and always taking anything out of shows that was the least bit naughty. They insisted that Verdon replace the word "pee" with "tinkle." Opening night Verdon said "Ooooh, I have to pee." After the show Ernie Martin came rushing backstage to Verdon's dressing room and said, "Gwen! You said *pee!*" Verdon looked at him in dismay and said, "Oh shit, I forgot."

(In Fosse's early shows, he also kept raising the key and changing the tempo, but sometimes he would be at a loss as to how to bring the number to a satisfactory conclusion. He used to ask us, "Does anyone have any idea how to end this thing?" One time I told him about an old World War II movie I'd seen starring Veronica Lake. She played some kind of spy, and at one point she bravely walked toward the enemy lines with a live grenade in her bosom. They didn't shoot her because they thought she was on their side. Just as she dropped into their foxhole, she blew herself and everything around her to kingdom come. What an ending to a picture! Sometimes Bob would get so frustrated he would turn to me and say, "Well, I guess there's nothing left to do but blow up the stage.")

Another great number was Roxie's "Funny Honey." Verdon began the number sitting on top of an old upright piano, singing about how she loves her wonderful husband, and taking sips out of an old silver flask. Her legs dangled just above the pianist's hands as the piano was rolled out on a platform from stage right. The number starts as a song of gratitude, because Roxie has convinced her husband that the man she shot was a burglar, and her hubby has agreed to take the blame. However, in the middle of the song, he finds out that the man she shot is her "friend" Fred, the furniture salesman. As her husband starts to be suspicious, and the liquor starts to make Roxie more tipsy, she begins to reveal her true feelings about her husband (which are not so loving). Meanwhile, she is dripping booze all over the piano player. Of course, all the time Verdon was singing, she was moving from one wildly sexy pose to another.

Roxie is accused of murder and has no money to hire a lawyer. She finally gets an idea and, during "Tap Dance," she "taps" her hubby for the money to hire the famous lawyer Billy Flynn. She is successful in her efforts, and Flynn decides to take her case. Flynn (Jerry Orbach) says he knows all there is to know about how to convince a jury. In the middle of this realistic scene he begins to sing "All I Care About is Love." The ladies of the ensemble appear out of nowhere and begin to assist him in their scanty costumes and enormous pink feathered fans. It was all very Busby Berkeley, and an outrageously funny idea.

Graciela Daniele played one of the many merry murderesses in the "Cell Block Tango." The other girls told their story in a very funny way, but her part was very sad and serious. She had to speak Hungarian in the role. The only two words this girl knew in English were, "Not guilty!" Fosse was pretty much leaving her alone in rehearsal, and she wasn't at all sure he liked what she was doing. She finally asked him what else she could do. Fosse turned to her and said rather coldly, "I don't know. I don't speak Hungarian. You look pretty guilty to me." Of course he did this to get a reaction from her. Daniele felt Fosse was a brilliant director. In the musical she played the first female in forty-seven years to be found guilty of murder. After the verdict comes in, she hangs herself in her cell. When Fosse spoke to her that way, Graciela suddenly knew how this woman must have felt, not being able to be understood by the jury. When you hear her plaintive voice pleading, "Not guilty!" on the original cast recording, it breaks your heart. Even though Fosse did most of the numbers as if they were part of an ironic and humorous vaudeville show, there was a dark and cynical edge to the piece.

Later on Verdon did the number "Roxie." When I saw the show I felt it was the epitome of what a great number should be. It started with Verdon looking at a newspaper, talking to herself and to the audience in a very funny soliloquy about her life and the fix she is in. There is the vamp of a double bass as she moves to the beat and expresses her hopes and fears. Near the end of it she suddenly realizes that she may at last be able to fulfill her lifelong dream of being a star in vaudeville. She calls on her boys (as she calls them) to come on and help her show the audience just what a wonderful number she will do. And as she sang and they danced together, did she ever show us! Gene Foote said Fosse told the boys to act as if they were watching themselves in the mirror. They were never to look at Verdon and they were to think to themselves, "I'm the best-looking man in the world." Verdon is master of the humorous but sexy move. She has all the intensity, but she can also be very subtle. I always feel she knows how each move looks from every seat in the house, and she finds just exactly the right angle for every step.

Chita Rivera was also sensational. Not only is she a powerhouse, but her style and her extensions are always incredible. Her "When Velma Takes the Stand" was another showstopper. When I saw the show opening night I could not figure out how she did the last step. One minute she was facing front standing on top of a chair, reaching for and looking up to the sky; and the next beat she jumped down into a backbend ending up lying with her back across the seat of the chair. It seemed physically impossible to do—but she did it, and the audience went crazy. Fosse inspired people to do the impossible.

When the show opened in Philadelphia on the pre-Broadway tour, some of the reviews were not too terrific. Fosse sat the cast down and gave them a great speech to encourage them and boost their morale. He also added, "Don't forget that the critics like to build someone up and then put them down. Last year I got the highest accolades, the triple crown, so now they're going to try to squash me. But, we're going to be so good, we aren't going to let that happen." And they didn't. The show was a smashing success.

Dancin'

ancin' opened March 27, 1978 at the Broadhurst Theater. It was a beautiful mosaic of the work of Bob Fosse. I think it was also his love letter to dance—and to dancers. By this time he had such a reputation for being brilliant that he had his pick of the best dancers in New York. And he could really pick them. He got the crème de la crème. Christopher Chadman and Kathryn Doby were Fosse's assistants and Chadman also performed in the show. The show featured Ann Reinking, Gail Benedict, Sandahl Bergman, Karen G. Burke, Rene Ceballos, Wayne Cilento, Jill Cook, Gregory B. Drotar, Vicki Frederick, Linda Haberman, Richard Korthaze, Edward Love, John Mineo, Blane Savage, and Charles Ward. The two alternates (who played a very important part in keeping the show in top running order) were Christine Colby and William Whitener. I list them all because for the first time ever, every single dancer got listed in the program as *starring* and each name was on the window cards in the front of the theater.

It was produced by Jules Fisher, along with the Shubert Organization and Columbia Pictures. Fisher also did the incredible lighting for the show. Fisher had worked with Fosse many times before, and they were definitely on the same wavelength. I believe they both wanted to do a show where they had complete control over what would ultimately be seen on the stage.

Although there is no listing in the credits for a writer, I'm sure the few times in the show when someone did speak or there was a voice-over, those lines were written by Fosse. However, the list of the people who wrote the music and lyrics is as long as your arm. Many of these composers were from bygone eras, and I'm quite sure none of the ones who were still alive were about to tell Fosse how to stage their songs. At last Fosse could work on a show where he didn't have to contend with the book writers or the composers. As John Mineo said, "It was a show that came totally out of Fosse's own head. At the same time, he was extremely willing to take what each person's unique personality had to offer." He did collaborate with the marvelously creative Ralph Burns, though, who did the orchestrations, and Gordon Lowry Harrell, who arranged the music. Both men had collaborated with Fosse before on other shows. So what we had was an example of the evolution of every kind of wonderful number that Fosse had developed over the years. As Chet Walker (who joined the cast after the first two years and stayed for three and a half more years) said, "He showed us his own style of American musical theater dance. He not only had his own unique diversity of style within that style, he also had the ability to show us the music within the music. Each number was like opening a Fabergé egg to see a three-dimensional story with a beginning, a middle, and an end. This was what his passion was about: dance, theater, and art."

There were so many wonderful numbers in *Dancin'* that it's hard to pick out only a few to talk about. Almost every number in the show would be a showstopper in any musical.

The show opened as Wayne Cilento came on from stage right, moved to center, and read from a sheet of paper: "The Surgeon General has determined that the viewing of too many musical comedies with sentimental and over-romantic plots may cause serious and sometimes incurable damage to the playgoer's and the critics' standards. Therefore, what you are about to see is an almost plotless musical. There will be no villains tonight, no baritone heroes, no orphanages, no Christmas trees, and no messages. What you will see is dancin' . . . dancin'! Some singin', and more dancin'! Ladies and Gentlemen . . . we hope you enjoy our dancin'!" and with a flourish of his hat, the show was off to the races.

Now usually a show about dancing would start with a big, splashy opening number with everybody jumping madly about. But Fosse never did the obvious. Also, it is hard to introduce each dancer as an individual that way. Fosse began the "Opening" with one lone girl (Sandahl Bergman) entering from upstage right. Without music she calmly walked to center, turned front, and slowly walked downstage. Then she began the first section, called Prologue, to the music "Hot August Night" (words and music by Neil Diamond). Using beautifully pulled-up legato movement, she danced a combination of balletic and modern movement stretched out to the nth degree. Slowly the audience was introduced to two more dancers, then three.

Fosse began to add a few more dancers at a time. The audience was really able to see each person. The dancers all looked very serious. They were told they should be looking straight front, as if they were watching themselves in the mirror. The number of dancers began to grow until all of a sudden the entire company was on stage each lit in their own overhead special spotlight. Together they took a deeply inhaled breath as they slowly lifted their arms up to the sides like wings. Jules Fisher's lighting was also growing brighter, directing the audience's attention. It was always obvious where Fosse and Fisher wanted you to look. Then as the tension grew Fosse started catching accents in the music with different rhythms and flicks of the hands. The music kept intensifying until the tempo crashed into the rock beat of the second section of the "Opening," called Crunchy Granola Suite, which also used music by Neil Diamond. As the lights bumped up, the dancers' hands sprang out to their sides, their fingers splayed open with their elbows held tightly in to the body. Everyone crouched down and all eyes changed focus to look directly at the audience. In that one instant there was a big smile on every face. Also on the downbeat, the dancers' hands began to quiver and their bodies began to pulse. Fosse told them to think of that moment as if the mirror had just broken into a million pieces, and they could suddenly see the audience for the first time. Out of all this seriousness came a mischievous playfulness that seemed to say, "we were just kidding." It was a stunning transition into a sensational rock number. The "Opening" seemed to be a celebration of what it means to be a dancer. Fosse always picked dancers who were not only highly trained in many kinds of dancing but also very capable of expressing emotion. This number had many different moods in the music, and Fosse got his dancers to feel them all, from humor and power to ecstasy; the movements revealed so clearly what they were feeling. This number had the most rehearsal, but just before the show opened in Philadelphia Fosse cut and edited his own work down to a fine essence. He wanted to be sure the audience knew just where he wanted them to look. John Mineo said there was a thought process behind every step. Fosse told them to always be an actor first, then a dancer. When Mineo and Reinking did the Broadway musical *Over Here*, they told me they knew how to shape their characters because of the previous experience they'd had working with Fosse on their acting.

The number that followed the "Opening" was called "Recollection of an Old Dancer," using the song "Mr. Bojangles" by Jerry Jeff Walker. This was about an old-timer (played by Chris Chadman) who admired Mr. Bojangles so much that he used his name. He danced in bars and fairs for drinks and had been picked up for drunkenness and disorderly conduct. As he sang about his lost youth, his dog who had died, and his lost agility, he danced a raggedy old soft-shoe. Behind him his young spirit (played by Gregory Drotar) also danced, but with total control, in the way the older man remembered performing when he was young. It was what all dancers go through as they get older and watch their technique fade away. The old man's grieving was touching, and the contrast with his younger self was very poignant.

"Percussion" closed the first act and I was really impressed by it. The number had four parts and was about how dancers, who love to express the different emotions each instrument in the orchestra evokes, especially have the hots for percussion. Part I was done by three girls to the claves and the triangle. It had very lovely legato floor movement and was done mostly as a round.

Part II was for three guys who each made his entrance by jumping off a trampoline in the wings and landing in a roll onto the stage. This section was accompanied by disco bells, tambourines, cymbals, snare drums, electric piano, and tom-toms. It was very playful with lots of shadowboxing, cartwheeling, and leapfrogging. Fosse used the three butchest guys for this dance. At one point, one man slid through the legs of the other two as they stood one behind the other with their legs in a widely spaced, turned-in second position. It was highly humorous in a very carefree, masculine way.

Part III had all the conga and bongo drums plus the cabeza and the queeza (which sounds like someone is sawing wood). This dance had a very Latin, mambo feel to it and involved all the dancers. A few of them were smoking cigarettes, and naturally Fosse even choreographed the smoke. The dancers used many different comical walks. One was done with swayed backs on half-toe doing back bumps. As the dancers moved along with their arms held way back in a curve towards their rears, they also exhaled on the beat. This dance had a very flirty, hot feeling to it. Near the end the dancers faced upstage, took off their hats, bent forward, put their hats on their backsides, and looked at the audience from between their legs on the last beat.

Part IV was to "Ionisation" by Edgard Varèse. It was a man's solo, and backstage the dancers nicknamed it the dance of death because it was so hard. The terrific Charles Ward did this originally, and Fosse had him do almost every difficult step it is humanly possible to do. It had every percussion instrument in the book in it too, and the wonder of it was how perfectly Fosse captured the sound of each one in his choreography. (The fellow who introduced the last section listed all the many percussion instruments that were in it. Then he added, "and some very heavy breathing.") At the end of the dance, Ward simply put up his hands and said, "That's all, folks."

The opening of the second act was called "Dancin' Man." The music was "I Wanna be a Dancin' Man" by Johnny Mercer and Harry Warren. Way off to one side in the program in very small print it said, "For Fred." Of course Fosse meant Fred Astaire, whom he greatly admired.

When the curtain came up, the whole company stood together in two lines holding their hats in front of them and not moving. The men and women all wore cream-colored suits, pink shirts, pink socks, white shoes, white gloves, straw boaters, and striped ties around their waists as belts (a la Astaire). The shiny black marly floor suddenly became white as it reflected the dancers' light costumes. In the beginning they barely whispered the song. The feeling was almost a prayer: "I wanna be a dancin' man, while I can." Slowly they began a small sway, side to side. This ode to the style of Astaire also investigated the many sounds that can be made with claps, slaps, and footwork, and was interspersed with short, surprising stops in the rhythms.

After an opening section with everyone, the dancers split in the middle and went offstage, leaving just a trio who did a number using the sand dance steps. Then four dancers came on while the trio danced off. (The backdrop was made up of spandex louvers that could be stretched open with the hands and stepped through.) As more dancers entered, the number began to grow and pick up in energy. Five dancers in the center did many slap combinations while four couples and two single performers were all doing different combinations around them. The intricacy of the many rhythms was electrifying.

Then, as the lights dimmed down, the dancers settled down to a big section of clap triplets using the knees and the hands, led by Christopher Chadman. He started very slowly, and after eight triplets two more people joined in, then two more, until at last everyone was clapping. The tempo and tension slowly picked up until it was going like a house afire. Then there was a big climax in the orchestration, the lights bumped up, and with great relief the dancers broke into some great jazz combinations. The number ended with everyone once again doing soft, small movements as they returned to singing and slowly left the stage. Finally only Chadman remained. He reached up as though to pull the chain on a light switch. As he pulled it down with a tiny gesture, the stage went black.

A number that was cut was called "Big City Mime." It showed the darker, seedier side of city life with con games, hookers, and massage parlors. The producers didn't like it and they had an out-and-out fight with Fosse about it. This time the producers won, so unfortunately we'll never get to see that one.

In Act III, one of the audience's favorites—and mine—was "Benny's Number," to Benny Goodman's "Sing, Sing, Sing." Fosse's program note was, "For Gwen and Jack. The latter would have hated it." (Meaning of course, Gwen Verdon and Jack Cole.) Well, if Cole had hated it, he would have been wrong! Verdon told me that it was not true, Cole never would have hated it. Anyway, it was fabulous.

The bandstand was upstage center, with the drummer elevated in the middle so everyone could see his solos. Fosse told the dancers that in the beginning of the number they should feel as if they were at the end of a long night of partying; then they slowly wake up and decide to have one last big blast. The men in their zoot suits and big hats, and the girls in their sexy, shimmering dresses slit up on both sides all looked incredible.

In the first section, the entire company was doing jitterbug steps: kicking, twisting their feet and shaking their hands, jumping in jeté with bent knees, or leaning sideways as they leapt into the air. Then they'd slide into wide fourth position and do double head-rolls. In the next moment, two dancers at a time did turns on their knees, while others walked wide-legged while pecking with their heads, and still others did side kicks. Then all the dancers suddenly took stop-tempo poses. From there everyone went into a fast energized ending, landing in splits except for two guys who crossed each other in big jumps. No matter how internally motivated Fosse was, he also wanted to make things bigger than life. He was not above going for the glitz and spangles, if it made for good showmanship.

During the Trombone Solo, as the lights dimmed down, there was a girl upstage center with two guys hidden directly behind her. All had their arms raised in a graduated sequence to look like an East Indian goddess with six arms. This section had a dirty-dancing feel to it way before anyone ever heard of dirty dancing. Only difference was, instead of a couple, this was a ménage à trois. At the end the girl hung by her knees over the arms of the boys, who were holding each other's shoulders. She contracted up to stroke their chests as they all exited stage right. Then a typical Fosse clump of people came moving across the stage—with writhing arms and legs, as always, coming out of everywhere.

As they cleared the center, and the Trumpet Solo began, Ann Reinking was revealed on the platform. She was leaning back, sitting sexily in profile. I've been told that every night at the five-minute call, Reinking would wash her long hair so it would look sensational for this number. She kicked up one leg, then the other, then turned on her hip to face front with her legs to the side. She let one leg drop off the platform to be in a sort of side swastika. Putting her weight back on her elbows and bringing her legs forward and off the platform, she repeatedly crossed her ankles keeping her hips in a straight line from her shoulders all the way down to her toes. (Of course, it doesn't hurt that her legs start under her armpits.) She did some sexy walks downstage and every few steps she threw her hand and head to the right as if she were getting rid of something. Later she did one jump with both knees up, into another jump, opening one leg to the front while backbending with her arms thrown back. She then repeated this sequence all the way across the stage and back again. She ended by running upstage as if to do a jump into a knee slide up on the platform, but instead she turned in midair to land facing front with one leg in back and one leg in front. After a big fan kick and some sensuous overhead arm movements, she left the platform to run toward a guy who was waiting to catch her up over his head on her back. While in the lift, she did one more kick and arm throw and then he ran with her to the wings, and for the ending of that section he thrust her one leg and one arm around some rungs attached to the back of the proscenium arch. She just hung there until the lights went off on her—and all I can say is, Oh my God!

The next section, called the Clarinet Solo, had four couples doing some nice, rather easy jazz moves as a relief from Reinking's solo. At the end the guys were on their backs, lying on the stage with their legs together up in the air. The girls spread the guys' legs and stepped between them to stand over the bodies of the guys. Then, as the girls closed and stretched open the guys' legs behind them, the guys reached up to stroke the girls' thighs. Quite an amazing sight.

Following this was the Piano Solo. Wayne Cilento and John Mineo tap-danced to this section with some very intricate steps. First the piano would play and they would answer with the same rhythms in their taps. Cilento and Mineo used tight, quiet taps, and the number had a very controlled feeling to it. Fosse began as a tap dancer, so he really knew what he was doing. Coming out of this section the piece opened up to end with everyone in a big, jazzy finish. Fosse not only knew how to make the choreography perfectly reflect the feeling of the music, he also knew how to make the hills and valleys dramatic and dynamic. To me this was Fosse's quintessential jazz number.

The finale of the show was called "America," and a grand finale it was. Before the number began, Bobby did a voice-over using various quotations by famous people about America. Each quote pointed up the many ways he felt about his country: amusement, disapproval, dismay, but also definitely love.

It started with the company in a very slow march singing "I'm a Yankee Doodle Dandy." As the singing grew more and more passionate the patriotism was obvious. On the final lyric, "I am that Yankee Doodle boy," the number evolved into two women and one man (Linda Haberman, Gail Benedict, and Gregory Drotar) who came out doing a spirited Irish jig (music by Gary Owens).

An amusing section consisted of a trio of women performing to the song "Give Me Some Men Who are Stout Hearted Men." They came skipping on very seductively. Here Fosse made fun of some American women's ways of acting babyish, flirty, and coy. Then out came a trio of men and Fosse did the same for American men's tendency to be super-butch, to fight, and to act macho.

Another pointed jab at prejudice in this country started with the music to "Dixie." A couple of black dancers come marching out. They heard the music, turned to each other questioningly, and said, "Is that *our* music?" After they decided it must be, they began to sing the song, making slight changes in the lyrics: "I'm *glad I'm not* in the land of cotton, old times there are *best* forgotten, look away, look away, look away, Dixie land." Then they proceeded to dance (wonderful split leaps and extensions) with great verve, style, and humor. Fosse was always controversial. Never ho-hum. People either loved that part of his work or hated it.

Next, Ann Reinking sang and danced "When Johnny Comes Marching Home." Her exuberant kicks and sliding runs had more energy than you can possibly imagine. She made the audience feel all the joy she would have when her lover came home from the ghastliness of war. At the end of the dance she crouched down for a moment. As she slowly rose and sang the last two lines of the song, we felt all her fear that perhaps Johnny would never return. Her passion and strength were awesome.

The last section in "America" was called Yankee Doodle Disco, and it was choreographed by Christopher Chadman. This wonderful opportunity happened because Fosse saw Chadman fooling around and experimenting with some steps and said to him, "I saw you dancing around, and I like the way you move. Why don't you choreograph a number?" Fosse gave him a month. When he came in and showed him what he was doing, Fosse loved it and put it into the show.

One of the reasons Fosse was able to get such wonderful performances out of people was because he would take the time to talk to them about how to develop into the best they could be. He made them feel he really wanted them to be great. Ann Reinking told me how Bobby advised her to get ready for a performance. He said, "Rehearse yourself more than you think you need to. Do your research. Be able to say no to yourself when it's still not good enough. Sit alone in the dark for five minutes and subjectively visualize the entire number. Do the very best you can. Then if it doesn't work, you can still go on, and you can learn from it." Good advice for any endeavor.

In the bows for the show Fosse really showed how much he cared about his dancers. Everyone had a separate bow and as each one came dancing out,

Dick Korthaze announced his or her name. Behind them was a large screen, and with each bow we saw film of that dancer, dancing. If anyone knew what it meant to be a dancer, it was Fosse, and he wanted to be sure that for once each individual was acknowledged.

Big Deal

*A*fter *Dancin'* opened, Fosse spent the next year writing, choreographing, and directing his incredible autobiographical film *All That Jazz*. Four years later, *Star 80*, his film about the murder of a Playboy Bunny, opened. Then another couple of years went by before he at last came back to Broadway to start work on *Big Deal*.

The show opened at the Broadway Theater on April 10, 1986, with Jules Fisher as the executive producer. It was presented by the Shubert Organization, Roger Berlind, and Jerome Minskoff, in association with Jonathan Farkas. Bob Fosse was not only the director/choreographer, he also wrote the book, based on the movie *Big Deal on Madonna Street*. Like *Chicago*, *Sweet Charity*, and *Damn Yankees*, this show is about a bunch of underdogs.

Fosse had the rights to *Big Deal on Madonna Street* for eighteen years. He kept meaning to do it, but one thing and another kept getting in the way. One day he started looking it over again and decided to do a reading. He used the actors Jerry Orbach and Roy Scheider (among others) and they, of course, were wonderful. That convinced him to do it.

Once again Fosse stitched a score together from some of his favorite old songs rather than bringing in a composer. Bob's standards were so high it sometimes made it difficult for him to collaborate, especially if he felt someone wasn't delivering what he needed. Fosse had good rapport with Cy Coleman, Carolyn Leigh, Dorothy Fields, Albert Hague, John Kander, Fred Ebb, and many others, but he'd also had many bad experiences with composers. I think he used the tried and true songs in order to avoid any unnecessary tension. Nevertheless, songwriters who saw the show told me that sometimes they felt let down when a scene led up to the moment for a new song and the strains of an old standby would rise from the orchestra pit instead.

The film *Big Deal on Madonna Street* was set in Italy, but Fosse decided to cast black actors in the leads and set the action in his hometown of Chicago during the Depression. Cleavant Derrick played Charley, a fast-talking ex-fighter, now gang leader, whose dream was to be the brains behind a big robbery. The humor sprang from how badly the job was bungled. Loretta Devine played Lilly (a naive maid to the people about to be robbed), and Charley's love interest. Alan Weeks played Willy, and Desiree Coleman played the ingenue, Phoebe. The beauty and range of her voice when she sang "Happy Days Are Here Again" were unbelievable. The two fabulous actor/dancer/singer/narrators were Wayne Cilento and Bruce Anthony Davis. The other four guys in the gang who were in on the big-deal robbery were Kokomo (Gary Chapman), Otis (Alde Lewis Jr.), Slick (Larry Marshall), and Sunnyboy (Mel Johnson Jr.). Valerie Pettiford and Barbara Yeager were the two shadows in "Me and My Shadow" (in which Gary Chapman doubled as Dancin' Dan), and Bernard J. Marsh was both the Judge and the Bandleader. Every single performer, including those in the ensemble, was outstandingly talented. Fosse could really pick them. The voices of the principals were to die for, and even the ones that weren't really dancers moved (because of Fosse) as if they were.

Fosse said, "*Big Deal* is about five guys struggling to pull a job. The struggle's like mine. I'm fighting my own indifference, my own cynicism. That's always been a battle for me. It's about fumblers trying to do something bigger than they ever thought they were capable of doing, and *never giving up*. That thread appealed to me—the desire to keep trying all the time. The reason I'm doing it now is that it's different from what I've been doing. It's not just straight dancing. It's the chance for me to do a story again. *And* it's sweet. Most of the stuff I've been doing is kind of hard-edged and cynical, particularly the movies I've done. *Big Deal* is certainly not cynical. It's sweet and funny and innocent. I always said to Cleavant, 'That's my part! A swaggering bumbler who thinks he's a ladies' man, and he's not. But, he keeps trying and covering up.'"

By this time, putting on a musical was getting so outrageously expensive that very few shows had out of town tryouts anymore. That's where the creative mettle of your staff is tapped, where audiences reveal what works and what doesn't, and where there is time to work out the flaws. *Big Deal* did not go on tour.

Usually on the first day of rehearsal everyone sits at a big table and reads through the script, looks at the set and maybe a few props, and then breaks for lunch. Not this time. Fosse said to the dancers, "Everybody put on your knee pads and let's start dancing." They'd all heard that he was a hard taskmaster and they got pretty nervous, but Fosse was not going to waste a minute. In the beginning he was very nice, and he went out of his way to make sure everyone was taken care of, but with every week that passed he got more demanding. One day near the end of rehearsals, when he was very tense, he said to them, "I've never been so disappointed in an ensemble in my life. I want you to know, it's not too late to make changes." He could be very difficult when he wasn't getting what he wanted. The cast was wonderful, though, and gave him everything they had. Some of the dancers told me it was the best work experience they'd ever had, and they were not upset with Fosse at all. He told them, "I can't wait around for you to begin doing your best. I want one hundred percent and I want it now." And he got it.

All the while they were rehearsing at the Broadway Theater, workmen were renovating it for *Les Misérables.* This was not only noisy, but it also probably made Fosse apprehensive about how much confidence the powers-that-be had in him. Fosse kept saying he wanted his stuff to be new, and he told some of the performers he was worried that he didn't have it in him anymore. In rehearsal he made a million changes, and one of the dancers asked him, "Why do you keep changing everything? Are you nervous?" Fosse looked at the kid in amazement and nodding his head up and down he said with a little laugh, "Yeah!"

Although the show did not have a long run, every number was worth the price of admission. There were three—some nights four—showstoppers. The show opened with Loretta Devine high up on a platform in a dramatic spot, singing a torchy version of "Life Is Just a Bowl of Cherries." She reprised the song at the end of the first act and again at the end of the show. (At Fosse's memorial at the Palace Theater she sang it again. Her voice was superb. The lyric "Don't take it serious, life's too mysterious," seemed especially appropriate as something Fosse would say to all of us.)

The two narrators then set up the show, dancing as they sang, "Most men hustle day and night, grabbin' money left and right . . . for no good reason at all," immediately revealing the gist of the show. Throughout, Fosse used not only the narrators but all the dancers to underline and emphasize the story line. He made the musical move cinematically. Everything he'd learned doing film came into play. The cross-fades between scenes were seamless, something amazingly difficult to accomplish on stage.

Another great number in the show was "Ain't We Got Fun," in which all the dancers were dressed as convicts. It was a big group because Fosse used the girls (disguised as men) too. The scene was a prison, and the performers were a chain gang. The chains connecting their handcuffs also dropped down to connect the shackles around their ankles. Sometimes the dancers became extremely frustrated in rehearsal as they tried to dance under those circumstances. They rehearsed this number endlessly. Many of them said they had trouble because putting on chains made them feel so oppressed and confined. One day during a rehearsal led by the dance captain and the assistant choreographer, one of the guys blew up and threw off his chains. He looked as though he were about to have a small breakdown. Phil Friedman, the stage manager, quickly came forward and said, "OK everybody, it's time for all of us to take five." I worked with Friedman many times and he was always there when you needed him.

Once the number got in front of an audience, though, the dancers realized it was really very funny. The stage lit up underneath to look like a grid, and a platform with sand on it slid on. The prisoners have been doing a forced fast march, but the guard finally gives them some free time. They proceed to do a sardonic sand dance on the platform, accenting their steps with the noise of the chains. They sang in a very slow tempo: "In the morning, in the evening . . ." (a long pause in which Lloyd Culbreath would do a slow, sad take to one of the other convicts and then look back out at the audience). Then they all shook their chains and he sang, "Ain't we got fun?" The audience roared. Fosse was incredibly inventive in the way he interwove the rattling of the chains, the tap steps on the sand, and the lyrics.

To me the best number was "Beat Me Daddy Eight to the Bar." All the dancers were in it, but it featured Wayne Cilento and Bruce Anthony Davis. They were both so good, you didn't know which one to watch. After a bit of milling about, the number really got started when everyone went into a tight group in the center, all reaching up with outstretched fingers. The hands all quivered as they slowly came down. For a couple of counts of eight the dancers slowly spread out and then the two featured dancers, Cilento and Davis, contracted up, one by one, to begin their part. The two guys wore caps and had suspenders with open vests over their shirts and pants. Boy, were they hot! They did a great staccato dance with lots of syncopated rhythms, using kicks and jumps and shoulder shrugs, and even snapping their suspenders to catch the beats. In contrast to their sharpness, the moves of the group behind them were languid and sexy, catching the accents, though in a softer mode. Gradually the whole group grew stronger until all the men danced together doing lots of knee work with marvelous strength in the line of their bodies. They did knee walks while opening their arms slowly above their heads, and even jumped in circles on their knees. (I bet nobody forgot their knee pads in that number.) You definitely got the feeling they knew and enjoyed the fact that they were arrogant small-town hoods. Near the end the women joined in and the whole group began to dance together. After many jazz turns and much fast footwork, everyone ran way upstage right in a clump and then, turning quickly, came flying back down toward the audience for a dynamic jump at the finish. Opening night as this number ended, the audience would not stop wildly screaming and applauding. They kept shouting "Encore! Encore! More! More! Do it again!!" The audience really wanted them to repeat the number. Wayne Cilento and Bruce Anthony Davis fell over on their backs to show they simply didn't have the strength to do it again. If you missed this number, it was performed on the 1986 Tony Awards telecast. You can still see it on videotape at the Lincoln Center Library. The people in the audience at the 1986 Tonys were also beside themselves as they whistled and clapped their approval. Fosse once again won the Tony for best choreography. He was still the master when it came to doing showstoppers for Broadway. I don't remember which critic it was, but one of them said "When you see a dance like this one, you know *Bob Fosse is back on Broadway and it is definitely a BIG DEAL!!*"

"Me and My Shadow" (with Gary Chapman as Dancin' Dan and Valerie Pettiford and Barbara Yeager as the shadows) was another wonderful number. It was done in the trio mode a la "Steam Heat" that Fosse loved so well. Stephanie Pope, who understudied the number, said that Fosse was so well prepared he made you want to give at least 110 percent all the time. He knew exactly what he wanted, but still he wanted you to make it your own. She said, "I'd heard all the stories about how hard he could be, but he allowed me to express myself and always gave me a reason for doing the movement. He treated all his dancers like actors. After working with Fosse I thought, nothing else will ever come close to this. It really felt good on my body, like I was home."

The second act opening was "Now's the Time to Fall in Love." It had some very erotic, sexy movement in it, and had a whole long section in which each guy in the gang revealed what it was he loved. Some sang about how much they loved a woman, others about how they loved their food, and still another sang and danced about how he loved his baby.

Alan Weeks sang "Everybody Loves My Baby" while holding his infant son in his arms. After sweetly singing the song through the first time, he started some very quietly sensitive tap a cappella. Slowly it began to build as the orchestra snuck in underneath. Then the two narrators joined him and the number really began to pick up speed and get exciting. And during the whole thing, Weeks made you believe he was really holding in his arms a child he truly loved. Fosse never forgot the love or the humor in a script, things that are missing from so many scripts today.

Toward the end of the show, in the middle of the robbery, each man has a daydream about what he will do with all the money they're about to steal. One of the funniest was Otis's (Alde Lewis Jr.) "Hold Tight, Hold Tight" about all the wonderful seafood he will be able to afford to eat. Lewis was one of many great tappers in the show, and he did a lot of the number up on a tiny table. It's hard to believe he did all those complicated rhythms in such a small space. For a dynamite finish, he fell backward off the table into the arms of the four ladies who backed him up in the number.

The producers wanted Fosse to change the ending of the show. They thought it was too dark. This seemed to happen in many Fosse shows. He wanted to entertain us, but he wanted to show the serious side of life as well. I thought the ending was perfect. When the gang is trying to break through the wall that contains the safe, they break into a water pipe by accident. Then they blow out the wrong wall. Finally there is a gas explosion, and they still don't have the money. They give up at last, and everyone leaves except Otis and Charley. Charley says, "So the deal fell through. But so what, there's always other deals, and I sure gave it one hell of a try." No wonder Fosse identified with that part.

How did some of the people in the show feel about working with Fosse? Loretta Devine said, "He engendered the magic of being the best you can be. He lets you go all the way. He lets you try, and then if you go too far, he'll pull you back." Cleavant Derrick said, in *Playbill*, "Getting a chance to be in a show like this is a gift." Stage manager Phil Friedman said, "I get spoiled working with Bobby because he's really in a league by himself. There isn't anything in the theater that he doesn't know or can't correct or give notes on. He's a perfectionist, and sometimes it's hard because we don't live in a perfect world. But that's part of his genius."

Each time I went to see the show I was afraid I'd run into Fosse and he would see how badly I was limping. It was just three months before I had both my hips replaced. I needn't have worried. He would have understood because he was in pretty bad straits himself. When he was interviewed four days before the opening, Fosse said, "If I had it to do over again, I'd have done more classical dancing, like Robbins. God, it's too late now. I can hardly move. I can't even tie my own shoes." He was suffering from sciatica and low back pain, but you'd never have known it. He just wouldn't let up. Strapped into a foam back-brace he whispered, "I love this show. But I gotta admit, it's a killer."

Epilogue

As I sit here writing and thinking about all of Fosse's shows again, I realize some of the factors that made him so successful, which today's choreographers and directors might want to take to heart. He had a special ability to give his performers images and a subtext not only to the script, but also to the lyrics and the movements. He also had humor, inventiveness, and the ability to edit his own work, simplifying down to the true line, so the meaning was clear. He had fierce dedication to doing his homework, and most of all he had that wonderful style.

Sweet Charity was revived very successfully in 1986, with Debbie Allen playing Charity. (Later on in the run, Ann Reinking replaced Debbie Allen. Then when the show went on tour, Donna McKechnie took over the lead.) Gwen Verdon did an incredible job of putting the whole show back together. Fosse came in periodically to rehearse the company and oversee the production, but he was very busy because *Big Deal* was in rehearsal at the same time. *Big Deal* opened on April 10, 1986, and the revival of *Sweet Charity* opened April 23, 1986, so *busy* was definitely an understatement. It is almost unheard of to open two Broadway shows so close together.

I want to tell you what Verdon, McKechnie, and others told me about the last rehearsal Fosse had of *Sweet Charity* before the company's Washington, D.C., opening. This was for the tour after the Broadway run in the fall of 1987. Everyone who was in the show remembers that day. They all said Fosse was full of life and

73

bursting with energy. He took off his hat (Fosse never went anywhere without a hat), and putting it on a seat in the audience, he went to work.

He had them do everything full out—about seventeen times—while he went over the subtext and nuance of every move. Fosse always rehearsed everything over and over so you would feel totally at home with the movements by the time you had to perform them. I wish more choreographers would do this kind of constant repetition. This rehearsal he seemed, even more than usual, intent on communicating exactly what he wanted. When they were really warmed up and in a good sweat, he sat them all down in the audience. They had been rehearsing "Rhythm of Life" and he said he wanted everyone to be so enamored of Big Daddy it would be like going up to that big drum station in the sky. Everyone said it was almost like he knew it was going to be his last chance to talk to them, and he couldn't seem to get the ideas out fast enough.

At first he talked about how they were doing the show and how to make it a success. He said, "You can't be out there selling the tickets. All you can do is just the best damn show you can do."

Then he began to talk more paternally about how they should be living their lives. "Remember to save your money, and take good care of yourselves. Don't be petty or compete with anyone on stage. Just make your own performance better. Try to be not just a better performer, but a better person. Remember when you are faced with a choice, or you have to make a decision, to think about what really matters and what is the important thing to do." Later he added, as an afterthought, "This past summer was the best summer I've ever had." To say the very least, it was an unusual talk for him to give before an opening.

The rehearsal ended and the cast was dismissed rather suddenly when they realized it was almost time for the half-hour call before the show. Only Verdon stayed on to show the drummer a couple of things he had to catch in "If My Friends Could See Me Now." As Mimi Quillin (the dance captain) left the theater through the audience, she happened to exit down the row that held Fosse's hat. Mimi told me she had seen that hat hundreds of times before but for some unknown reason that day she stopped and rested her hand for a moment on top of it. She said it was as if she was waiting for it to give her something, as if she could absorb something from him just by touching his hat. Maybe she felt something magical might happen because she was so in awe of Fosse. The next day she thought a lot about that moment.

At one point Verdon looked up to see the stage manager talking with someone way upstage in the dim light. She wondered who he was talking to.

Suddenly she realized with a start that it was Fosse. He looked so ashen and gray she hadn't recognized him. As he started to leave Verdon ran after him to catch up. I think Verdon sensed something was wrong. She told me he said to her, "I'm just going back to the hotel for a while before the opening." Verdon said, "Wait. I'll go with you," and they walked off together toward the hotel talking about the opening night party. Fosse said, "I wish Nicole was here." Gwen said, "Me too." Fosse said, "Because Nicole loves parties."

Verdon and Fosse were about halfway there when he suddenly stopped and said, "Hold me, I feel dizzy." At first they both thought it was a petit mal epileptic attack. Then it seemed to be a grand mal seizure. Finally when Fosse collapsed on the ground, they realized it must be a heart attack. Verdon called out desperately to strangers to get an ambulance. Finally somebody got one there . . . but Bob Fosse died on the way to the hospital.

That night, no one could understand why Fosse didn't come back at intermission. After the show there was an announcement over the intercom asking everyone to come on stage. Everybody thought, "Oh no, maybe we're going to close." They all came downstairs and gathered together at the side of the stage and one of the producers finally said, "Bobby died." No one knew who he was talking about. They all were asking, "Bobby who?" Only the people who had known Fosse for a long time called him Bobby. Then they said, "Bob Fosse. Bob Fosse died this afternoon."

Many of the men in Fosse's family died rather young of heart trouble. I'm quite sure this contributed to the darker side of his personality. Donna McKechnie told me he once said to her, in a very off-hand manner, that he thought about dying all the time. Some have said Fosse was very self-destructive and wanted to end it all, but many other people told me it wasn't true, that he definitely wanted to live.

Fosse was an exceptional and fascinating man. Although he was a master at manipulating and controlling his performers, he did it in order to get what he wanted for the show, and we always knew he really cared about us. He treated his dancers like actors, and thankfully he never called us kids, as so many do. He always addressed us with respect and made us feel we were important to the success of the show. In my experience, he was as close as you can get to a genius, both as a director and as a choreographer. We will never stop missing him.

Thank God, Verdon was with him. If anyone could have been a support to him at that last moment, it was her. She was his best friend, and I'm sure it was meant to be that they would be together at the end.

When Leslie Bennett interviewed Fosse for the *New York Times* just before the opening of *Big Deal,* he said, "There are forty-three scenes! It's like

World War III trying to do this thing!" But he also said, "There is always one's immortality to consider. There's something about trying to create something that gives people pleasure. Something about camaraderie. Maybe somebody will remember you." Then he added rather softly, "Maybe somebody will say ... He was a good showman, he gave us good shows. You could always count on him for an evening's entertainment."

We sure could, Bobby.